FACING TYSON

FACING

TED KLUCK

TYSON

FIFTEEN FIGHTERS
FIFTEEN STORIES

THE LYONS PRESS
GUILFORD, CONNECTICUT
AN IMPRINT OF THE GLOBE PEQUOT PRESS

Copyright © 2006 by Ted Kluck

The Lyons Press is an imprint of The Globe Pequot Press

10 9 8 7 6 5 4 3 2 1

Printed in the United States of America

Library of Congress Cataloging-in-Publication Data

Kluck, Ted A.
Facing Tyson : fifteen fighters, fifteen stories / Ted A. Kluck.
p. cm.
ISBN-13: 978-1-59228-919-6
ISBN-10: 1-59228-919-3
1. Boxers (Sports) I. Title.
GV1131.K58 2006
796.830922--dc22
                                            2006022145

For KRISTIN,
I love you so much.

CONTENTS

My main objective is to be professional but to kill him.
—MIKE TYSON ON LENNOX LEWIS

Acknowledgments		ix
Introduction		xiii
Chapter 1:	**Mike Tyson**	3
Chapter 2:	**Sam Scaff**	19
Chapter 3:	**Mitch "Blood" Green**	33
Chapter 4:	**Marvis Frazier**	43
Chapter 5:	**Jose Ribalta**	59
Chapter 6:	**James "Bonecrusher" Smith**	73
Chapter 7:	**Pinklon Thomas**	87
Chapter 8:	**Tyrell Biggs**	109
Seconds Out:	**The Larry Holmes Interlude**	129
Chapter 9:	**Tony Tubbs**	133
Seconds Out:	**The Peter McNeely Interlude**	149
Chapter 10:	**Buster Mathis Jr.**	153
Chapter 11:	**Evander Holyfield**	169
Chapter 12:	**Steve Lott**	187
Chapter 13:	**Lou Savarese**	199
Seconds Out:	**The Andrew Golota Interlude**	211
Chapter 14:	**Lennox Lewis**	221
Chapter 15:	**Kevin McBride**	233
About the Author		243

ACKNOWLEDGMENTS

To WRITE A BOOK is to be grateful. First, special thanks to my editor Tom McCarthy at The Lyons Press, who from the scads of grizzled boxing writers—men who are older, wiser, have seen more, done more, been bled on more, waited more, and interviewed more—picked me, a relative kid, to write this book. This was fun, and I learned more about boxing, the city, families, and people on this project than I ever knew before.

To Cyberboxingzone.com editor Stephen Gordon for giving me my first opportunity to cover live boxing and for your vast library and network of online resources. To the International Boxing Research Organization and Dan Cuocco in particular for helping me make important connections. Additionally, *Blood Season* by Phil Berger was used extensively to provide places, names, and contexts for the interviews that follow. Boxrec.com was used for fight results, ring records, etc. *Shadow Box* by George Plimpton and the *Book of Ecclesiastes* were both used for encouragement.

To Jeremy, a fighter, and Becca in Brooklyn for a place to sleep, great food, and even better conversation. To Stephen, another fighter, in Upland, for the coffee and encouragement. To the friends—Chris and

Beth; Jen and Jon; Craig and Beth; Detta, Sara, and Zandy; Evan and Jenny; Jim and Sandie; Knitter and Beeg; Kevin and Trisha; Ruthie; the "D" group; Beezer and Bridget; Jeff and Catha; the URC high school Sunday schoolers—who provided much needed conversations about real life (things besides boxing, books, and sports). To Rich and Bonnie for lunch, a warm bed, and perspective in Atlanta. And to my parents for all of their unconditional love and support.

To the managers, promoters, and trainers who gave of their time and contacts to this project—Mike Acri, Ziggy Rosalski, Dennis Rappaport, Bob Spagnola, Jeff Cummins, Ken Schick, Packi Collins, Courtney Myers, and especially Bruce Kielty, the Grand Rapids matchmaker, for his kindness and patience. More than once I fought the urge to tell him that he was too good for this sport. The same could be said of Steve Lott, whose stories are so good that he really ought to write his own book. To Meka Bennett, who saved my interview in Atlanta, and Ashley Smith, for returning my calls and setting things up with Lennox. You both have difficult jobs that you do very well.

To Kristin, who is an integral part of everything—things much bigger than boxing books—good in my life. It was your hard work and sacrifice that gave me this opportunity. And to Tristan, age three, who would tell anybody within earshot that his daddy was writing a book about Mike Tyson and that tomorrow Mike Tyson was coming to our house (still hasn't happened, but the invitation is still good).

Finally, to the fighters for their courage in the ring. What you do is unique, and, in spite of what I say and think about your sport at times, I have a great deal of respect for all of you for being great and, now, for being ordinary with dignity. Thank you for letting me into your lives.

And to Mike, you distinguished yourself while most of us never register a blip on the world's radar. For a time you were the best at what you did. You fought courageously in victory and defeat, which is all anyone can ask of a professional boxer.

INTRODUCTION

Michigan seems like a dream to me now . . .
I've gone to look for America.

—SIMON AND GARFUNKEL, "AMERICA"

THE MOST ENJOYABLE PART of this project has
been the conversations—not only with the fighters,
but with regular people in airport terminals (too
many—the terminals, not the people), hotel lobbies,
restaurants, and elevators. They ask what you do.
You tell them you're writing a book about Mike
Tyson. He's a lunatic, they say. What an animal. An
icon. A freak. Did he try to bite your ear off? Ha ha.
They all say this as if they were the first people clever
enough to think of it.

I especially enjoy the look of shock on their faces
when I tell them that I found Tyson to be kind, gentle,
accomodating, and intelligent. Well read. Good to children. A guy who seems to want to live out his years
quietly, but, as per American celebrity culture, will
probably never get the opportunity. Their shock, I
think, is my favorite part. That, and the travel. This is a
book that happened from the inside of cars . . . rentals
. . . airplanes . . . airport shuttles . . . riding to see people
who may or may not show up. People who once were

televised and now aren't but are now remarkably like us. Regular. It's about Tyrell at 57th and Haverford in Philly, Lott on 5th Avenue, Tubbs still in the ring, Pinklon in the diners, Marvis in his dad's shadow. Me in my dad's shadow and extremely proud to be there. And about finally taking her with me to Miami.

She had asked me why was it again that I like boxing, which is something she asks pretty much every month. I talk about how it's human drama, how there is more respect for the opponent than in any other sport, and how I've met some of the most open, honest, and interesting people covering boxing. I then talk about how I'd like to get back in the gym, maybe do some light sparring. That's usually when she throws something at my head.

"It's the brain damage I have a problem with," she says. "I have trouble with a sport where the idea is to concuss the other guy."

It's hard to argue with that. I've felt ill at ringside before, and some of those experiences are described in detail on these pages. Boxing ravages the body. It is a head-trauma sport. I had always tried to rationalize it away before, telling people that if guys got out at the right time they would be fine. That is not true. Every man who has stepped in the ring has come out a little less whole. I used to think I wanted to do it, to box. But I've since learned that it's like being a war historian. You become an enthusiast, you go to the museums, watch the films, you respect the men that bled and died, etc. But at the end of the day you're glad you're glad you weren't there, dodging the bullets. Such is my relationship with boxing.

Watching Mike Tyson walk into a boxing ring in his prime was akin to watching Barry Bonds hit a home run or Michael Jordan shoot a basketball. Or maybe it's more like watching one of those mushroom clouds billow up during a documentary about "the bomb." It's a thing of such ferocious beauty that you can't force yourself to look away. At any rate, Tyson was the Picasso of the ring walk. He had it down to such an extent—with the gladiator-themed garb (towel, black shorts, no socks), frightening physique, and blank stare—that he often beat men (see Michael Spinks) before the fight even began. Regardless of how one feels about Tyson's body of work as a whole, especially in recent years, he mastered the ring walk with brutal style.

Mike Tyson was, and is, a cultural icon. In his heyday, before his loss to Buster Douglas, he was a box office draw and marketing commodity of Jordanesque proportions. This is a Tyson who punched often and with no wasted motion. A Tyson who showed head movement and didn't pose after punches. The punches themselves were physics lessons delivered with a maximum of bad intentions, as he liked to say. This, despite the high voice and lisp, still managed to sound really scary. He was an antihero before the 90s made antiheroes cliché.

My goal was to learn more about him by interviewing his contemporaries—the men that walked into the ring with him and opposite him and survived. I tried to talk to these boxers, managers, and trainers in their own environments—their homes, their gyms, and their streets—and hear each tell the story of their brush with the "baddest man on the planet." Some of his opponents went on to fame and fortune in the ring (Evander Holyfield, Lennox Lewis); others, as is often the case in boxing, have ended up back on the streets.

This is not meant to be a definitive chronological history of Mike Tyson, or a thinky, sociological treatise on "how the streets made Mike the way he is," but rather an opportunity for the greatest storytellers in sports—fighters—to tell their stories. That said, boxing is a hungry man's game, and many of his contemporaries proved difficult to pin down. Many refused to talk with me because there was no money in it for them; at least two (Cliff Etienne and Henry Tillman) are behind bars for violent crimes. Razor Ruddock, according to one prominent manager, is on the lam in Jamaica trying to evade the long arm of the IRS. Tony Tucker asked, "What's in it for me?," which could be the battle cry of our generation. Peter McNeeley, at the behest of his manager Vinny Vecchione, needed $500 bucks because, as he said, "We're just a couple of hardworking guys trying to make ends meet." I am inclined to believe him, but we never connected. Buster Douglas was working on his own book, and feared overexposure. After several good conversations with Jim Kurtz, manager for Bruce Seldon, his fighter passed—it was too hard, he said, to reopen that chapter of his life. And the vast majority, it seems, just disappeared. There is no player's association to keep them together, and there is no banquet circuit for the ex-boxer.

THE BOOK HAS PROVIDED some enduring memories—fearing for my life in the back seat of Pinklon Thomas's car, being sold on the travel business by James "Bonecrusher" Smith, arguing over the breakfast bill with Kevin McBride (he wouldn't let me pay), and being drunk-dialed by Mitch Green on my cellular phone. Yes, I have changed my number. Perhaps the most memorable event was being there for the end of Mike Tyson's career on June 11, 2005, in Washington, DC.

I knew I was going to write at length about Mike Tyson on June 8, 2002, the night he lost to Lennox Lewis in front of the whole world, losing the fight, along with much of his mystique, in an 8th round KO. I was covering a small fight card in Mt. Pleasant, Michigan, with my father, doing a short piece for ESPN.com on then-heavyweight title contender and current IBF champion Chris Byrd. The gist of the piece was that Byrd is the anti-Tyson—a soft spoken, genial family man who reads the Bible and for whom boxing is just a sport, rather than the definition of who he is. All of that, by the way, is very true. Byrd and his family were delightful. He knocked a guy named Jeff Pegues silly and then hung out with his wife, parents, and kids backstage. The whole thing was about as sinister as a church picnic. Then, on giant televisions set up in the casino theatre, my father and I watched the dismantling of Mike Tyson.

I had never felt much for Tyson before, other than the fact that I felt like my childhood, in a boxing sense, was defined by Iron Mike. Like many, I had lost respect for him as a result of the rape trial and his other public foibles and, if pressed, would have admitted to rooting for Lennox Lewis that evening.

Tyson walked to the ring accompanied by the fierce beats of DMX, complete with towel and entourage, looking menacing and looking like Mike Tyson. Strangely, as Tyson's entourage got bigger, his performances began to suffer. The ring in Memphis (Tyson had already been expelled from the boxing Edens of Las Vegas and Atlantic City) was filled with yellow-jacketed security personnel, forming a human wall between the entourages of Lewis and Tyson in the ring. At that very moment there was perhaps no more posturing to be found on the entire face of the earth. There was much strutting and shouting. And then Lennox Lewis proceeded to dismantle him over the course of eight painful rounds. I found myself feeling sorry for Mike Tyson in the way that you feel sorry for someone who is on the brink of losing much of what is important to them in life. I saw a very frustrated Tyson in the corner between rounds, a Tyson who didn't want to continue taking the beating but who fought on courageously. When the knockout finally came in round 8, I found myself strangely depressed, having watched my generation's boxing icon reduced to two ghastly cuts and a knockout. Yeah, Tyson was a thug, but he was our thug, and that was significant. He would, as he said in a famous, much-parodied post-fight interview, "fade into bolivian."

My dad mentioned something about feeling the same way when he watched Larry Holmes and Leon Spinks beat up Muhammad Ali. My father wasn't an

Ali fan. He sided with Joe Frazier when the nation took sides back in the early 70s. You were either an Ali guy or a Frazier guy. My dad was a Frazier guy. But even the Frazier guys were saddened to see Ali honor the time-tested boxing tradition of staying in the game too long. It was those beatings, and the accompanying sparring sessions, that helped leave Ali in the shape he's in today. Tyson, sadly, seemed to be walking the same path.

That night, driving home from the casino, was the first time I prayed for a professional athlete. I prayed for Mike Tyson because I knew that the years ahead of him were not going to be easy. Mike Tyson is a man who lived his whole life in the pursuit of human appetites—money, sex, fame, power—and in the end found them all to be lacking. This, I think, must be the epitome of hopelessness.

Of late, Tyson's public life has become the train wreck from which we can't turn our eyes. Though he hasn't won a meaningful fight in years, he still sells out arenas, and in the same interview he alternately speaks of feeding his heart to his opponent and talking to Jesus. I grew up in his era. I played his video games and watched his fights, usually wanting to see him lose, but, recently, rooting for him in the way that one roots for nostalgic figures whose character flaws have gone remarkably public, while most of us manage to keep ours private. Mike Tyson has been many things (heavyweight champion, armchair philosopher, accused rapist), but he was, and still is, if anything, interesting.

But America wants Mike Tyson to die.

In our culture we have no mechanism in place for larger-than-life celebrities growing old quietly. They have to die young (Elvis, James Dean), be hurt to such an extent that we can eulogize them while they're still around but can't ruin their own legacy (Muhammad Ali), or, sadly it seems, they have to take their own life. When Curt Cobaine did insane amounts of heroin and shot himself, the enlightened talked about what a folk hero he was. Kids cried, college students lit candles and wrote bad poetry, professors with ponytails taught courses on What It All Meant. When journalist Hunter S. Thompson took his own life, my own sometime-employer ESPN.com devoted page after page to essays on what a brave man he was for "going out on his own terms." As if reaching a point of hopelessness is a path anyone would choose.

Mike Tyson's last rebellious act needs to be living out his years in quiet contentment. Living well for Tyson will mean disappearing. Enjoying his family, enjoying his friends, flying his pigeons. This will be his last statement in the direction of the media and the general public, both of which I am a part. I wish him the best in this important endeavor.

FACING TYSON

CHAPTER ONE

MIKE TYSON

*I don't mean to sound unsympathetic to
your plight/
But if you're really so shy/
Why are you standing in the light.*

—PATTERSON HOOD, "CAT POWER"

TYSON TRAINER JEFF FENECH is a thick-necked, good-humored man wearing a sweatshirt emblazoned with his own Fenechs boxing gear logo. His company distributes boxing gloves and ring apparel, and he has built a reputation as a world-class trainer. Fenech, a former lightweight champion of the world, is completely at ease. Oddly, at a professional fight it is often only the fighters and the ex-fighters who have nothing to prove. Everyone else, from the pimps and players in the concourse, to the closet-case tough guys in cutoff shirts, to the hair-gelled little PR wonk, has a gigantic, almost tangible chip on his shoulder. The fighter, by comparison, has already done his proving.

Fenech is asked what is unique about his man, Tyson. The two have been working together only a few months, but have been friends for much longer. Tyson's high-profile trainer divorces read like a who's who of boxing, from Kevin Rooney all the way up to Freddie Roach. I am expecting to hear stories about training, about how we are going to see glimpses of the old Tyson. He shares the following story.

"Mike and I were flying into Washington, DC, for this fight [Tyson vs. Kevin McBride], and were seated in first class—seats 1A and 1B. I sat down and started reading, and when I looked up there was a little African-American boy in my seat. I said to him 'where's Mike?' The boy had never flown first class before and Mike gave him the seat and then just slipped away, back to coach."

IT's EASY TO SPOT fight people a mile away— they're the ones that look out of place in a swank hotel lobby. The guys in the shirts with the cut-off sleeves, the guys that wear a Brooklyn Dodgers jersey and backwards hat to a nice restaurant and don't care. When the fight world descended upon Washington, DC, for the Mike Tyson vs. Kevin McBride fight, they changed the tenor of the place. Make no mistake about it, the circus was in town.

There's a little Italian man in front of me at the hotel desk. He is joking around with the pretty young black girls at the desk—he doesn't know how to use his camera phone. Can you show me how to use it? Ha ha. They love him. He's short, but he's an older guy with a young face, which is exactly the kind of older guy I hope to be someday. I run into him again at the bank of elevators.

"You ready to go tomorrow?" he asks, as if I am fighting or training a fighter tomorrow.

Oh, I'm just watching tomorrow, you?

"Working the corner of Chris 'The Mechanic' Smith."

Wow. How's your guy? He ready? We banter the easy boxing banter that happens in an elevator the night before a fight. When the circus that is boxing descends on a town, it's like summer camp for a few days. Summer camp with booze, broads, and violence. I ask his name, as he looks vaguely familiar. He is Joey Gamache, the not-so-old fighter. A fighter from my childhood who is now training, who had a great career, but is more famous for losing a hard fight to a blown up Arturo Gatti. Funny that we are both here because of a fighter from my childhood who is still fighting.

"You know I used to be Tyson's roomate?" Gamache offers. He waves me into his room, where his wife is already in bed. She pretends to be mad at him— she already has the moisturizer on her face for God's sake—but sits up in bed and is an active participant in our interview. It is 11:45 P.M.

"He's [Tyson] a good guy. I hope he can turn it around. I think a lot of people are rooting for him now. It's not all his fault."

The Tyson legend has become a piece of American sporting and cultural lore by now. The hardened ghetto kid, born in Brooklyn in 1966 to Lorna Tyson and Jimmy Kirkpatrick, is arrested for purse snatching at age 12 and is subsequently taken in by an old white ascetic and trainer of champions Jose Torres and Floyd Patterson, Cus D'Amato. D'Amato shares his philosophies on boxing and life while teaching the kid to harness his ferocity and in the process become the most marketable figure in a sport that makes money only when its figures are marketable. The ascetic dies and the kid is left to fend for himself. In that sad prodigy way, most prodigies aren't equipped to fend for themselves—they are best coexisting with their benefactors. He makes bad choices. He is taken advantage of. He finally becomes a cautionary tale, or an example of All That Is Wrong with Boxing. Or he is an inspiration, depending on who you ask.

Tyson's redemption has become something of a hobby for the nation. People either want to see him climb back up the ladder and put his life back together, or they want to see him utterly destroyed, because the only thing America loves more than success and celebrity is seeing people dismantled. There's a lot I still don't know about boxing, but I'm pretty sure the destroyer won't be Kevin "The Clones Colossus" McBride. McBride is a big man, six foot six inches and 271 pounds, and is billed as the "heavyweight champion of Ireland," which is probably akin, no disrespect intended, to being the heavyweight champion of Kentucky or Ohio. Unfortunately, he is as ponderously slow as he is large. To make matters worse, McBride has fought nobody of note—his biggest victory coming against another plodding Irishman named Kevin Montiy. McBride seems like a genial bloke—his thick brogue coming through in every interview. He makes the obligatory white-man's attempt at trash talking in pre-fight press conferences. He tells the world that Tyson is going to feel all of Ireland when he punches him in the ring, which sounds quaint and nice when he says it, like the false bravado of a man about to go to the gallows. The television executives hope that all of Ireland buys the pay-per-view at $44.95 a pop. McBride also openly admits that he has a hypnotist in his camp for this fight. Destroyers don't hire hypnotists.

Tyson, for his part, promises a "train wreck," but appears only mature, honest, and introspective in his pre-fight media interviews. Clearly his heart isn't with this noise. This is Tyson the father. Tyson the middle-aged man with regrets. This is a Tyson we can relate to, which isn't always good—for us or for a man about to fight for money. This is a Tyson whose career has been in decline since he parted ways with Kevin Rooney, after knocking out Michael Spinks in 91 seconds in 1988. After that there were other trainers and other wins, though those inside the sport saw Tyson as beatable as the old vestiges of the D'Amato style began to fade.

Even Tyson's trash talk seems contrived now. He mentions something in a pre-fight press conference about "gutting McBride like a fish." The Tyson camp releases the usual pre-fight video clips of Tyson stalking around the ring, working the hand pads (Tyson training footage, I think, is some of the most impressive video in sports—they will be dusted off in future decades as examples of raw power and intensity) or exploding around a heavybag. The general public is convinced that he will, indeed, gut McBride like a fish, or something close to it. People want to see that. They want to see the past restored and return to an era of predictability—when the economy was thriving and Mike Tyson was knocking out everything in front of him.

"He was vulnerable," says Gamache. It's late and I am beginning to feel guilty about intruding upon his hospitality. I wish him luck with his fighter, and he walks me to the door while trying to sum up his connection to Tyson.

"We came from the same kind of background, with no money. When you come from that, you spend every minute feeling like the wolf is always knocking at your door. You never feel comfortable or safe."

Kyle, I'm sorry I sucked tonight.
—MIKE TYSON, WHILE SIGNING AN
AUTOGRAPH FOR A CHILD, POST-FIGHT

IN THE SPAN of about 30 minutes, the same crowd that cheered Mike Tyson lustily is booing and throwing garbage on him as he exits the floor of the MCI Center. His own people are in the process of selling him down the river. I happen to be standing in the lower concourse next to the Irish bagpipers who accompanied McBride into the ring, as he confidently waved the Irish flag before the fight. They're a small lot of older Irish gentlemen with gray hair and distinguished-looking beards. They're the kind of guys who probably carry pictures of their grandkids in their wallets. I feel a surge of pity for them, for having to be there and witnessing the chaos that is big-time heavyweight boxing. They look as shocked as everyone else and are probably wondering if there will be a post-fight gig in it for them. I ended up watching the fight standing next to a tiny Hispanic woman who worked in foodservice at the arena and had a kind face, but spoke very little English. She had wound her way through the throng and down the tunnel to get a closer look at the action, making these priceless, shocked facial expressions as Tyson slid further and further into ineffectiveness as the fight went on.

Tyson walked into the ring wearing a simple black T-shirt, without any of the music or bombast that accompanied his walks in the past. My memories were of the slit-towels, the stare, and the rap beats that used to accompany him. But then again, this is a 39-year-old man, and people mature—they outgrow things. While it may have been culturally acceptable to be overtly aggressive in 1987, eighteen years and a rape conviction tend to mellow one's approach.

"I just wanted him to concentrate on the fight," said Fenech of the decision to scale back Mike's ringwalk. "I didn't want him to worry about the walk or anything else. I wanted him relaxed."

In round 6 of his scheduled 10-rounder against Kevin McBride, Mike Tyson simply ran out of gas. McBride's strategy was brilliant—to weather the 15 to 20 seconds of old-Tyson magic that Mike mustered at the beginning of each round and to spend the rest of the round using his 270 pounds to lean on, hold, and generally frustrate the former champion. McBride started hitting him more often; Tyson punched less. McBride's strategy of grabbing Tyson's right arm as soon as he got close seemed to be working, as Tyson began to get frustrated, which drew repeated warnings from the referree. At the end of round 6, Tyson collapsed and slid down the ropes, more the result of a McBride shove than a punch. He stayed on the canvas, on the seat of his shorts while the ringside photographers, smelling blood, literally leaned through the ropes and swirled around him. He was the picture of a man defeated—slump-shouldered, exhausted, mouth open, breathing heavily. I turned to communicate my own shock to the Hispanic woman, but she had returned to work—no doubt somewhere preparing for the chaos that would come.

TYSON IS ASKED if McBride ever hurt him.

"Shit, every punch he hit me with hurt! My body hurts. Everything hurts. I'm going to go home and soak and hope I'm not sore in the morning."

This is a post-fight Tyson speaking at the press conference and later at a less formal affair involving about five of us, still holding our tape recorders. He is perhaps the most compact man I have ever seen in person. The distance from his deltoid (shoulder) to elbow can't be any longer than six inches, but it contains a huge mass of bicep bearing an image of Arthur Ashe and the words "Days of Grace." The bicep is encased in a casual shirt, and Tyson wears black slacks. His round face looks peaceful, despite the tribal tattoo he acquired on one side of it before the Cliff Etienne fight and the distinct little masses of scar tissue and swelling around his eyes. These are the trademarks of the old fighter—the kind that producers tried to manufacture on Terry Malloy in *On the Waterfront*. Incidentally, I saw white kids walking the concourse at the MCI Center with the same tattoo applied by marker to their pale faces.

The MCI Center swirls with backstage activity. Post-fight, there are those milling around, trying to get a glimpse at a celebrity, and those who are just trying to get out of there and get home after a long day and night of work. My feet are killing me. I realize that I have been standing for the better part of the day and slink over to a rolled up pile of floor mats to sit for a moment and collect my thoughts. Tyson is just a few paces away, on the dais, fielding questions about the fight.

Mike, why didn't you get up at the end of round 6? (Tyson was saved by the bell and eventually found his way back to the corner, where Tyson trainer and longtime friend Jeff Fenech stopped the fight.)

"I was tired. I didn't want to get up. Jeff [Fenech] wanted to stop the fight . . . we didn't want to stop. Jeff is a sensitive man . . . he's too sensitive with me. He was a great warrior and a champion but he's sensitive with me. Isn't that something?"

The answer is almost too honest and straightforward for any of us to understand at the moment. It is wildly charming, in a way. Fenech would say in a later interview that he vowed not to have to pick his friend up off the canvas that night. He promised the former Monica Tyson that he wouldn't let her ex-husband get hurt.

"I gave him a cuddle in the corner and told him it was all over . . . the other guys told me to let him fight, but I said this is my . . . expletive . . . corner and it's over," Fenech explained. "Then, without any prompting, Mike went over and congratulated McBride on a great fight. The Baddest Man on the Planet, one of the greatest heavyweights of all time. I was the most proud of that. Mike Tyson is a true sportsman."

McBride, who had made a tactic of grabbing Tyson throughout the fight, complained of headbutts and rough tactics. Tyson's response?

"Of course I was butting him. I'm a fighter. I was trying to win the fight. Shit. But I wish him the best in his career and I'm just glad that nobody got hurt. I don't love this anymore. I haven't loved it since 1991. When I came out of prison and won the titles, I just scared people out of the titles—I would walk into the ring and win those fights."

Why were you so good, he is asked, at boxing?

"Poverty," he says, without a moment's thought. "If you look at the champions . . . blacks, whites, Vietnamese . . . you know what they had in common, all of them? Poverty. They had poverty. When I was a hungry man, I wanted to fight, I wanted to be an animal, know what I mean? In 1906 when Battling Nelson said, 'I'm gonna kill that darkie and beat out his brains,' it took 30 days to get to New York. Now if I say something, in 30 seconds it's all over the world."

He is asked the inevitable questions about legacy. About what people are going to talk about. About the Hall of Fame.

"I felt like I was 120 years old out there tonight," Tyson continued. "I'm not the fly guy anymore. I'm not the guy with the jewelry and the big fleet of cars. This isn't in my heart no more . . . I don't have it in me to get in the boxing ring again. I hate the smell of the gym. I don't like this business and I don't like the people in this business."

Tyson went on to retire from the fight game that night, which may or may not last any amount of time, as this is, of course, boxing. He tells the throng that if he can't hang with a C-list fighter like McBride (his words, and he names McBride by name), he has no business getting in the ring . . . doesn't want to embarass the sport, etc. To all of this McBride nods amiably, happy to be there, as if in agreement with everything that Mike is saying. This, too, is bizarre. Tyson almost seems more comfortable in defeat than he has in victory in recent years, though the victories have been few and far between, with a quick knock-out of now imprisoned Cliff Etienne, in Memphis in 2003, and the Dane, Brian Nielsen, in 2001.

Most of the assembled media throng have left now, to wander the DC streets among the hookers and post-fight revelers—it's like they imported Las Vegas to Washington, DC, for one night only. Outside, happy, drunk Irishmen are dancing in the streets and picking fights with unhappy, drunk Tyson fans. It is an ugly scene. Inside, Tyson is speaking softly to a small group of reporters and hangers-on who have remained. Muhammad Ali has shuffled by and paid his respects after watching his daughter win impressively over Erin Toughill. Tyson's handlers said that

Ali was there, for quite some time, in the dressing room after the fight to comfort Tyson. Tyson seems at peace now and thrilled to talk about anything but boxing. He is asked whether he can enjoy and take pride in watching his old fights.

"I don't watch them. I can't. I hate the violent guy in those fights. I don't know that guy anymore . . . the guy that talked about pushing a guy's nose into his brain and talked about being the best fighter in the world. I don't have any connection with that guy anymore."

It is that Tyson, though, who is the inspiration for this book. The Tyson who thumbed his nose at amateur boxing and the Olympics to learn the sensational knockout style that would make him the richest heavyweight in the history of a sport, whose only moral code is the ability to generate gate and pay-per-view. It was the violent Tyson who waxed Trevor Berbick (and then Bonecrusher Smith and Tony Tucker) to unify the titles and become the youngest heavyweight champion in history, and who would celebrate in a gaudy coronation concocted by one Don King. He wore a crown and carried a scepter and, that night, met Robin Givens. It was that Tyson who walked into the ring like a gladiator and always walked out a winner. We saw him buy cars and mansions and felt like, in some way, we were giving him those riches. We were allowing a poor black kid from Brownsville the opportunity to taste the best that America had to offer. Black people loved him. White businessmen loved him. Frat boys loved him. We could count on his success and knew that whatever was happening in America politically, at least nobody in the world could whip Mike Tyson.

Tyson, then, buried Cus D'Amato and finally Jim Jacobs and parted ways with the remaining management that groomed him, kept him busy in and out of the ring, and helped him become, for better or worse, an American Celebrity. He married and divorced Robin Givens, went away for several years as the result of a rape charge, and when he came out was never the same. He was angrier out of the ring and worse in it. Instead of being a small, explosive, hard-to-hit heavyweight, he was instead just a small heavyweight. He floundered in and out of our consciousness long enough to knock out an inferior fighter in some faraway locale, and in the process say or do something apalling. The pay-per-view numbers were still amazing and have remained so. He bit a man's ear. There were studies. People who pontificate pontificated, and Tyson was analyzed from every conceivable angle. He was reinstated and then beaten soundly by Lennox Lewis with the whole world watching, and that, I think, was the end of Mike Tyson the fighter and the beginning of Mike Tyson, the piece of nostalgia.

He is asked, finally, about how he plans to pay his debt to the government, rumored to be upwards of $40 million according to some sources, without fighting. It is the elephant in the room.

"Shit, I don't know. If I get some money, I'll pay them . . . if not I guess they'll put me in jail, but at least I'll have a roof over my head."

The remaining group claps and some laugh. I'm not sure what we're applauding—his decision to not have a plan, his honesty . . . probably his decision to never fight again. It is our nature as writers to try to ascribe more meaning to people, especially athletes (see Muhammad Ali), than is actually there. I feel especially compelled to not make Mike Tyson a symbol for anything besides what he was—a great fighter who made some bad choices, got old, and then took beatings. He wasn't the first and he certainly won't be the last. And then, inevitably, the tributes start, making Tyson feel like an observer at his own funeral. He stops them.

"Look, I don't want no swan songs and I don't want nobody to shed any tears. I'm a cold, cruel, hard man. I don't know what to do when you cry . . . I just want to give something back. I want to be a missionary . . . go to the Sudan, help with the relief efforts. I've lived my whole life for myself up to now."

Tyson seems comfortable with the doctrine of sin at least, and seems to understand his own desire for redemption.

"I'm not the person I used to be . . . I mean, I'm still not an angel . . . I'm still lascivious, periodically [this draws a laugh]. I'm just trying to find some balance in my life. I don't like my work and I don't like the people in my work. I don't like that world . . . I don't want to live the life anymore where I party and try to get girls."

He is asked so many questions about how he would like to be remembered, when he wanted to quit. He looks exhausted and answers questions more often than not with "I don't know." It is a worn-out statement from a worn-out man. I feel like he is tired of sharing his life with us, and I don't necessarily blame him. We care until the next deadline, until we have to care about the next guy, in the next locker room. We'll miss him when we're interviewing the next cyborg athlete or coach, spinning out the next tired cliche.

There is a frantic search on for a permanent marker now, as Tyson would like to sign a fight program for a child. The journalists around him are screaming for a permanent marker. It's all pretty funny. It's late, and everyone is exhausted. And after a several minute search, Kyle finally gets his autograph.

There is a post-fight party down the street in DC—the usual affair with booze, loud music, hoochie clothes, and metal detectors at the door. These are the kind of parties that are more for the hangers-on than the actual fight people. The people who have better things to do are usually doing them at this hour. Tyson would not appear. The journalists can't believe he's just going home to take a soak. He has to repeat himself several times.

"Life isn't about what you acquire," said the fighter who was adopted by Cus D'Amato as a teen and became the youngest heavyweight champion of the world and perhaps the biggest draw in the history of the sport. "Life is about losing everything."

CHAPTER TWO

SAM SCAFF

Boxing is for men, and is about men, and is men.
A celebration of the lost religion of masculinity
all the more trenchant for being lost.

—JOYCE CAROL OATES, *ON BOXING*

I AM SITTING IN MY Toyota Echo, feeling the small-
ness of my vehicle more acutely than ever, at the
QwikFill in Raceland, Kentucky. I have been driving
the hills and valleys (past the same farms, used car
lots, and this QwikFill) of Raceland and the surrounding area for nearly an hour looking for the Sam
Scaff residence. Now, surrounded by drivers of F-
350's, Rams, and Silverados, I swallow my pride and
ask for directions.

Scaff, a huge man—six feet seven inches and over
250 pounds—greets me at the door of a home that
looks eerily like the one in which I grew up. It is mod-
est and Midwestern, decorated in a sort of feminine-
country motif. Not only is there nothing in the house
to suggest that Scaff was a boxer, there is nothing to

suggest that he lives there at all. After waving me in, he apologizes for not taking a shower before the interview, as he just got home from work. That's something else Midwesterners do—we apologize first and ask questions later.

Sammy Scaff is a fighter who boxing people often label a "journeyman." I learn that he has been a union pipefitter in Raceland since 1976. I will have to look up the exact work of a "pipefitter" when I get home. This is a problem. Writing articles and books about champions and chasing around arenas for quotes is a good way to lose touch with reality. I can tell you what the groupies and freaks were wearing at the last Mike Tyson fight, but I couldn't tell you exactly what a pipefitter does.

"I became an apprentice pipefitter in 1976," he says. "I loved boxing, but I worked nights and trained in the daytime, so I was always showing up at work tired, and showing up tired for training. I did it because I loved the training and loved the travel."

After what seems like an eternity looking in the basement, Scaff produces a Timberland boot box full of boxing pictures and clippings. We settle in at the Scaff dining room table for our interview. There are placesettings arranged decoratively on the table—pastel blue plates on woven placemats. It seems an odd place to interview a fighter. His kids' prom pictures adorn the wall—tough-looking, crew-cut Midwestern kids with heavily made-up girlfriends. It all looks extremely familiar. I was that kid once, and that was my girl.

"I don't look at this stuff much," he says matter of factly. "People ask me 10,000 questions about the

Tyson fight all the time at work and around town, they all know about it. I tell them I lasted longer than Marvis Frazier and Michael Spinks!"

Scaff is easy with a laugh and smile. He strikes me as the kind of guy who is at peace with his boxing career in terms of what he did and didn't accomplish.

"I started boxing at age 12 when I lost a street fight," he explains. "I got beat up, and one day my dad brought home a pair of boxing gloves and I was hooked. My dad always supported me during the amateurs, but never really took to pro boxing. I brought him with me once, to a fight in Atlantic City to work the corner, but he couldn't go through with it."

Scaff racked up a 75–5 amateur record, winning Golden Gloves tournaments and state titles in Kentucky and West Virginia. He was also growing into a very large man.

"I played football and basketball in high school, too . . . and basically had an agreement with my basketball coach that I could leave practice whenever I needed to to go train for boxing. Boxing is my first love."

The pictures are out now and we are looking through the memories of Scaff's life in boxing. Most of the pictures involve Scaff smiling at the camera with a giant cut or welt around his eye. There are also photos of Scaff in exotic locales, dining with South African dignitaries. The kid from Flatwoods, Kentucky, has gotten around.

"I started training real hard in 1981 and had my first pro fight in 1983 in Knoxville, Tennessee (a first-round knockout over Philip Manuel). I fought four former world champions and fought in Brazil, England, Bermuda, and South Africa."

We are looking now at a book of photos from South Africa. One, in particular, shows Scaff holding up a smiling black child.

"I brought this home to my parents and said 'I want to introduce you to your new grandchild.'"

Scaff looks up from the kitchen table to gauge my reaction before belly-laughing at his own joke. There are the race relations that you learn about in university, from well-meaning philosphers in ponytails, and then there are the race relations you learn about in the fight game. He produces a press clipping.

"I fell in love—head over heels—with a Lebanese woman on one of my trips to South Africa. They wrote about us every day in the paper. That was 1984. She was a Catholic girl . . . they would write headlines like 'American Fighter Comes After South African Sweetheart.'"

In the photos she looks beautiful and exotic, Scaff very much the big, American cowboy sporting sweatsuits and a Fu-Manchu mustache, which exists to this day. He talks with a slight lisp and what appear to be the effects of years of fighting for a living. Combined with the Kentucky draw, it gives him the appearance of being very sleepy, or at least makes him tough to understand.

"We kept in touch for a few years . . . writing and calling. But I've been married six years this September. Maybe that's why I haven't heard from her in a while!"

Another belly laugh—Scaff is rolling now. Our talk turns back to boxing and Mike Tyson.

"The Tyson camp called me in 1984 to come up to the Catskills and work as a sparring partner with Tyson, but I had a cracked rib at the time and couldn't do it. I ended up fighting him in the Felt Forum underneath Madison Square Garden in New York City on December 6 of 1985. I really didn't know anything about Mike Tyson, so I did what I usually do, which is meet the guy in the center of the ring. Needless to say he broke my nose and my corner wanted to stop it in the first round."

"Scaff had big balls," remembers promoter Mike Acri, a fixture on the Northeast boxing scene throughout the 70s and 80s and into today. "Sam was a tough guy who took fights on short notice, which as a promoter is all you can ask for. He's what people like to call a journeyman, but in reality he won a lot of fights and fought a lot of big names."

Journeymen earn their monikers because, largely, they are fighters without hometowns. They are the boxers who travel, often without cornermen, to take, and most likely lose, fights on short notice. These are the fighters that contenders use to pad their resumes and get quality work. I have seen these fighters, covering many small cards in the Midwest. They typically travel alone, or with one long-suffering trainer/father figure. They dress in small, poorly-lit cinder block rooms with drippy faucets. There are no fans screaming their names. They fight, probably lose, take their cash, and drive back that night, so as to save on the cost of lodging. Oddly, almost all of the men I have interviewed for this project ask about Scaff—they want to know where he is and how he is doing. He was a blip on the radar of most of their careers, but in some way he earned their respect.

Incidentally, there is something very satisfying about watching journeymen like Scaff ply their trade on the Midwestern circuit. For starters, you can get a ticket without spending a small fortune and sit close enough to the ring to actually see—and feel—what's happening inside it. This can be both good and bad. When the fights end, you can simply stroll out to your car, as opposed to jitterbugging through a crowded Vegas concourse, weaving through the throngs of pissed off (at least half of them) quasi-fight fans, only to navigate a labyrinth of slot machines before being regurgitated onto a Las Vegas street at 2 A.M., writing up a crap fight report and then staggering back to your hotel room.

SAM SCAFF FOUGHT in Las Vegas exactly one time—a loss to Mitch "Blood" Green in 1984. I'm in town to cover the Oscar de la Hoya vs. Shane Mosley rematch. Las Vegas is perhaps the most depressing place in the world tonight—the intersection between heaven and hell.

As I walk to the MGM Grand Garden arena for the fight, I'm passed by a Cadillac Escalade with a television in the back window playing a porn video. A group of frat boys on the sidewalk in front of me cheer wildly. I guess the late-80s push to make Vegas a "family friendly" town really didn't take. My peers in journalism tell me not to be "wide eyed" in print. They tell me not to be awed by what I see. I'm trying very hard, at the moment, to appear jaded and cool. As a journalist, appearing smug and detached is my job.

The migrant workers with brochures for hookers have their own cadence and marketing strategy—they slap the brochure (for young virgins, teens, preggos, horny older women, horny black women, etc.) on their thigh, slap slap, and then present it to you. As if the thigh slap is going to make it more appealing and make you forget that you are looking at someone who snuck across the border in the backseat of an old Nova that reeked of piss, dreaming big American dreams, only to get a job in Vegas peddling flesh for minimum wage. My head hurts.

Passing time outside the arena playing "guess the hooker" with some new friends I made from San Diego. They looked skittish and out of place, with a digital camera in a room full of celebrities, so I ambled over for a chat. Despite my credentials, I also felt skittish and out of place.

"We snuck past the guy at the door," they explain. "We do this at all of the big events." They snicker conspiratorially and glance at my press credential.

I imagine a small apartment somewhere with a huge plasma screen television and walls papered with photos of these people with their arms around bored and slightly confused looking celebrities. The thought makes me very sad.

"Hey, talk to our friend," they ask, shoving a cell phone at me. They have told their friend that they met a writer from *ESPN The Magazine* (me). I exchange uncomfortable hellos with the friend who is somewhere else in the building on a cell phone. Everybody talking. Nobody communicating. The fact that I do actually register on their celebrity Richter scale isn't nearly as cool as I thought it would be. Life for you.

There goes Tommy Lasorda with the CEO of Outback Steakhouse, or is it Texas Roadhouse? There goes Sean Rooks from the Clippers and that forward from the Celtics. There go a couple of hot, nameless women. Hookers, my friend decides. There goes Tiger Woods . . . Dennis Quaid and his son. This is the big fight atmosphere. The ladder of celebrity climbing higher and higher—the Stairway to Heaven, as Robert Plant may have called it. This, as a boxing writer, is what you live for. There are no celebrities on the Midwestern circuit—no embalmed C-listers making their way to their seat, painfully conscious of who may be looking at them. If there are celebrities in the crowd, they are most likely other fighters—there to watch their peers ply their trade.

My celebrity-chasing friends have cornered Sean Rooks for a photo. They wear ecstatic looks on their faces. Sean looks like a deer in headlights. Another photo to add to their wall. Mission accomplished.

I'm passed by a familiar figure. A blown-up fighter. A cat who used to be a small fighter when I was a kid . . . a guy who dropped off the radar about 10 years ago. He mumbles by, wearing a T-shirt and a gigantic, swollen black eye. I remember his features but can't place the name. He has the look of a former legend. He came to the right place. Vegas is the purgatory where former legends go to play out the string, after they die.

Nobody stops Iran Barkley for an autograph. Nobody knows who he is.

SOME JOURNEYMEN, like Scaff, are more quality than others. But against Tyson, it was quickly evident that Scaff was overmatched.

The tapes show a large, ponderous Scaff who is simply hunted down and destroyed by a younger, quicker, stronger Tyson. Tyson caught him with a left hook early in the first round and followed it with a right hand that landed flush. Scaff stayed upright, however, and succeeded in circling and keeping Tyson at bay with a jab, until being trapped in a flurry and knocked out at 1:19. Indeed, Scaff's nose, flattened to one side and gushing blood, is one of the more disgusting things I've seen in a professional life spent covering a pretty disgusting sport. To his credit, Tyson immediately rushed over to check on his fallen opponent, even embracing Scaff in spite of the volumes of blood that were pumping out of his nose with each breath. When Tyson turned back to walk to his corner, his face showed something between genuine concern and disgust. Tyson's upper back and shoulders were covered in Scaff's blood.

Tyson was 19 and not yet ranked. But nine of his first thirteen wins put his opponents to sleep before the end of round 1. His fight against Scaff was his first scheduled ten-rounder. And with all three major networks after him to make his television debut, Tyson's aggression was already becoming a commodity. Imbued in his mad rushes forward was an intricate style of slips and weaves that made him extremely elusive. And although his opponents were nothing special, the talent was there and Tyson was busy; he fought thirteen days before his bout with

Scaff (TKO 2, Conroy Nelson) and would fight six-teen days later (TKO 1, David Jaco). These fight films, the images grainy and raw, are similar only in that they portray a motivated Tyson stopping a variety of fighters in dimly lit gyms and arenas. His camp insisted on having each of his early fights videotaped, as they seemed to know the magnitude of the commodity they had on their hands.

Tyson was a throwback to an era in which heavyweight fighters fought and fought often. Above all, Mike Tyson was the picture of a man who fought for a living. "Cus D'Amato's basic philosophy," said the late Jimmy Jacobs, "was that whether you were a brain surgeon, pianist, or fighter, you've got to do it frequently to do it at your best."

"Not long after the fight, they offered me a thousand bucks a week to come up to the Catskills to live and spar with Tyson," Scaff recalls. "The rules there were that you made your own breakfast and lunch, and always washed your own dishes. Those were Camille Ewald's rules. I remember standing in her kitchen washing dishes with Tyson. We ran together and trained together. He was a nice guy, but was all business."

The Catskills home of Cus D'Amato and Camille Ewald was where Tyson spent the majority of his formative years under the watchful eye of D'Amato, after drawing the attention of a guard at the Tryon School (a juvenile detention facility) and being subsequently 'discovered' by D'Amato. There are stories of troubles at school (he was finally expelled from Catskills High School), but Tyson was raised by the two largely as a child prodigy would be raised. He trained during the days, his evenings were filled with boxing talk and fight films. It was here that Tyson became a student of the game.

Like his most famous charge, D'Amato was an enigma. He spent the bulk of his years at the Gramercy Gymnasium in Manhattan, sleeping on a cot in the back of the facility, with only a police dog for companionship. It has been written that he feared snipers and never married, as he never trusted a wife to not lead enemies to his doorstep.

"One night, it was the night before one of his fights, we were having dinner with Bill Cayton, Jimmy Jacobs, and Tyson. Well, right after dinner, in walks this drop-dead gorgeous black woman in a long fur coat. Tyson got right up and left with her. I said, 'What the hell is going on here?'"

Conventional wisdom and boxing lore suggest that fighters stay celibate up to six weeks before their fight. The boxing ascetic would suggest that the pent up sexual energy flows straight through one's gloved fist and into the other fighter. That all of the angst of sexless, lonely training can somehow be channeled on fight night. The moderate, however, thought the chase more damaging than the act itself.

"One of them, I don't remember if it was Cayton or Jacobs, said 'He's a young guy, he'll be fine.' I guess it didn't slow him down any."

Scaff's career spanned nearly a decade, and he fought, and lost to, many of the biggest names in the heavyweight division at the time. His name is present on many of their ring records, a blip in the universe of boxing history. A loss to Mitch Green in Las Vegas. A loss to Tim Witherspoon in Birmingham, England. A loss to Adilson Rodrigues in Brazil.

"Gerry Cooney's people offered me a thousand bucks a week to come out and spar with him," says Scaff. "But everybody knew that Cooney would work his sparring partners to the bone and then bring in the media and knock them out in front of the reporters. Cooney was kind of a dick. Fuckin' boxing's a crooked sport. I never took a fight to lose . . . I just don't believe in that shit."

Scaff's profanity is not laced with anger as much as it is just the language of the blue-collar Midwest, and really just the language of sports in general. I ask him more about the financial frustrations and ethical dilemmas he encountered.

"I fought on ABC's *Wide World of Sports* once, and that's at least a $40,000 payday. Don King was involved, and after the fight I didn't get my money at all. King was working with my managers . . . my managers made me pay for everything. Food, phone calls, everything. I remember another time when I was working a corner for a guy—they said, come down here and work with this guy and we'll pay you $5,000. Well, Don King walked up to me before the fight, told me he'd pay my guy five grand to take a dive because our opponent was a guy that King was trying to move through the ranks. I told King that I didn't go in for that shit, but that I'd pass it along and let my guy make the decision. When I told him about it he said, 'Oh yeah, that was my plan all along. I'm getting an extra $2,500 so I thought I'd just dive.' I got offered $600 bucks one time to take a short-notice fight in Dayton Ohio. They said they'd pay me the $600 if I lost. I said 'how much I get if I win.' They said 'nothin.' I didn't take the fight."

Scaff still trains periodically, doing situps on the deck by the pool, and walking, sometimes up to five miles per day through the Kentucky hills, which was a staple of his boxing-career training regimen. He also explains that he rarely watches boxing on TV, for fear that he'll be tempted to give it one last try.

"I took my daughter with me to my last fight. It was a long drive, about four hours from home, and I lost the fight. He came out and I hit him with some shots in the first round (his opponent West Turner was down twice in the round), but they just stopped the fight in the second after I got into trouble in one of the corners. On the drive home my daughter—she was about 14 at the time—said 'Daddy, please don't ever fight again.' That was my last pro fight." Scaff produces a picture of his daughter smiling in a hotel room—a souvenir from the last fight trip.

We are walking outside now, watching my son play with blocks on Scaff's driveway. It's hot out— Kentucky hot, about 95 in the shade, and humid. I am not at all surprised that Scaff's retirement was final. Not having much to base this on, I also guess that when people from Raceland, Kentucky, make promises to their kids, they keep them. I finally get around to asking Scaff about fame.

"I worked for 31 years as a union pipefitter. I enjoyed boxing for the travel and training, and the guys at work loved to ask me about it." He pauses. "I remember fighting once in Atlantic City, on the undercard of a big TV thing . . . there was a green room, and Larry Holmes and Sugar Ray Leonard were there. Those guys and me. It was crazy. I couldn't believe I was actually there. But those guys wouldn't talk to me—wouldn't even give me the time of day. I think it's because I was white."

He is offering drinks to my wife and son. He shakes Tristan's hand, comments on what a big bruiser he is. We exchange addresses, and I promise to send a DVD copy of his fight with Tyson, which he's never seen. He's never seen any of his fight films. Soon we are piling in the car and rolling out of the driveway. Fame never comes up again. Scaff offers a big wave as we pull out of the property, and hollers, "Don't forget me."

I roll down the window and shake his hand again, one last time.

CHAPTER THREE

MITCH "BLOOD" GREEN

*The state of boxing is the closest thing to
sixteenth-century buccaneering as there is on
the planet today.*

—SETH ABRAHAM, HBO

MITCH GREEN IS A living rap video stereotype.
Gold teeth. Check. Jheri curl. Check. As a writer, I
am acutely aware of the fact that I am treading on the
very thin ice of racial stereotype, but Mitch Green
looks like the kind of guy who would kill you for
your Nikes and throw the shoeless body in the dump-
ster. This makes me uneasy.

Mitch Green is famous for two things: (a) Getting
beat up in the ring by Mike Tyson, and (b) getting
beat up in the street by Mike Tyson. The latter happened outside a dry cleaners in Brooklyn on August
23, 1988—Green began talking smack with Tyson
about money he was owed by Don King, only to
come away with a fully closed, baseball-sized left eye
and five stitches to go with the erstwhile mop of hair,

gold teeth, and toothpick. Tyson himself did not escape unscathed, breaking his hand in the melee.

Tyson later said of the incident, "I guess I could have avoided it."

In the ring Green erred on the side of caution, although he was game, one of only a handful of men to have taken Tyson the distance. His strategy, like Bonecrusher Smith's later, would be to clutch and grab as much as possible. To his credit, Green looked to be in shape, without an ounce of fat on his tall, six-foot, five-inch frame—this in stark contrast to his flabby-breasted bretheren in the heavyweight division. Occasionally, as Tyson worked his angles and fired uppercuts and hooks in the direction of Green's mane of hair, a halo of sweat would cascade off into the distance, indicating to the crowd and judges that there was damage done. Although the pace of the fight was pedestrian, thanks mostly to Green's insistance on grabbing, it was not without incident. Green's other strategy seemed to be to spit out his mouthpiece whenever he became winded, which was often, starting after about the 3rd round. Every few moments, it seemed, Tyson was launching Green's mouthpiece out of his mouth and onto the canvas or into the crowd or press row; the highlight coming in round 5 when Tyson blasted Green with a hook, sending several teeth and a dental bridge rocketing into the audience. The television announcer Larry Merchant remarked that Green once had 120 men under his employ as a New York city gang leader, adding that he could use some of them in the ring that night.

Tyson would say of his opponents, "I try to catch them right on the tip of his nose because I try to punch the bone into the brain."

Green came by the nickname "Blood" as a result of his experiences in the street, where, as he put it, "I'd be making guys bleed." Green had gained some renown inside the ring as well, as a four-time New York Golden Gloves champion, and by compiling a 16–1–1 record as a pro. He was also ranked number 7 in the world by the WBC heading into his fight with Tyson at Madison Square Garden.

The other sidenote to this story was Green's conflict with Don King a few days before the fight. Convinced he wasn't being paid enough for the fight, Green went public with his thoughts at a Madison Square Garden weigh-in.

"They ain't been payin' me," he said, almost to himself. He went on to describe his agreement with Don King—namely that he fights for whatever King gives him, which is the reason why he wasn't fighting much.

"This man [King] isn't keeping my money anymore," he said, his confidence building. "He said he was going to do me right, and he hasn't." Green went on to threaten Carl King, telling him he was going to get paid "one way or another." Green, toothpick hanging from his mouth, was trying to summon every bit of street credibility he could muster. Unfortunately, he was trying to hustle the man that invented the hustle, Don King. Green would fight, and he would fight for $30,000—a pittance in boxing terms, once everybody takes their share. Though King had told him that he and Tyson were being paid roughly the same amount, Tyson would earn $200,000 plus another $450,000 from HBO, which televised the fight. Green would be released from his contract following the Tyson fight (L 10 in the record books), never to be heard from again.

I DIAL MITCH GREEN's cell phone number, and while it seems like there is an answer, all I hear is noise in the background. I faintly recognize the sounds of rap music. I get frustrated because cell phones are frustrating even without the added barriers of culture and, perhaps, the destructive effects of ring wars. I hang up. Seconds later the phone rings again. It is Green this time, and I can barely make out what he's saying. I explain the concept of the book—15 interviews with Tyson opponents, a chapter on each guy. He says he wants to get paid for the interview. Says I'm going to get rich and he gets nothing. Mumbles something. Yells something at someone else, off the phone.

I explain to Mitch that I can't pay him for the interview. That nobody is getting paid. That I would like to buy him lunch, at least, and give him the chance to tell his story via a chapter in the book.

"Lunch? Shit. You gonna get rich [again] and I get nothing." Green's diction is barely intelligible. I understand about a third of what he is saying on the telephone. Suddenly the prospect of a lunch someplace seems a little ridiculous. I imagine Green and I at a trendy Brooklyn bistro. I'll have the goat-cheese salad, and for you, Mitch? That type of thing. I try to change the subject.

"Where you working out these days, Mitch?"

"Gleasons."

Green fought once in 2002, beating a guy named "Experienced" Danny Wofford for something called the World Boxing Syndicate heavyweight title. Wofford had lost 94 times. But to his credit, on a few weeks' training, Green showed up and pounded out a 12-round decision. He also fought in 2005 in Tennessee (aka the land of the easy boxing license), but has been something of a double-edged sword for promoters—a name, but also a fighter with a penchant for pulling out of fights at the last minute.

"Why don't I plan on meeting you at Gleason's at noon on September 24?" I suggest. The idea being to meet in a public place. Very public. Alone is the last place I want to be with Mitch Green. To wit, an example of Green's reaction to the mere mention of Mike Tyson, from a 2002 article by Mitch Abramson in the *Village Voice*:

> He showed up at Madison Square Garden for the Golden Gloves finals and, of course, all hell broke loose.
>
> During an intermission between fights, the Daily News' Bill Gallo stepped into the ring to call up champs and celebrities, including Zab Judah, Mark Breland, and Sugar Ray Robinson's son, Ray Jr. All Gallo had to do was announce, "Is there a Mitch Green in the room?" The 6-foot-5 Green bounded up the steps and into the ring, shadowboxing from ring post to ring post. The crowd of 5000 went nuts. "Mitch Green, as you

*all remember, fought Mike Tyson twice!" Gallo
announced. "Once going the distance with him in
the ring, the other time with him in the street!"
Upon hearing Tyson's name, Green screamed at
Gallo, who added with a smile, "Both times he
lost!" Green started yelling into Gallo's micro-
phone, "And new . . . and new . . . ," referring to
his recently becoming a "world champion," but
Gallo probably didn't know what Green was talking about and ignored him. Green eventually was
dragged out of the ring and went back to his seat,
where he happily spent the rest of the night signing autographs for a line of fans.*

"Man, I ain't gettin' paid nothin?" Green continues. I tell him that I've talked to several others already—Sammy Scaff, Pinklon Thomas, Tony Tubbs,
and James "Bonecrusher" Smith. None of whom
got paid.

"Iron Mike? Shit, they ought to call him Cotton
Mike. He ran. Ran for 12 rounds [the fight was
only 10 rounds] . . . I try to get a rematch with him
and he takes me to court. So what do I get out of
this interview?"

"The chance to promote your documentary . . . "
I am reaching now. All out of answers for Blood
Green. I take a look around my office and realize
how normal my life is. I can hear the sounds of the
street behind Mitch, who is still convinced that boxing writers get rich. He laughs at my attempt to ap-
pease him. I tell him I would still very much like to
do the chapter.

"Call me . . . call me when you get into town," he says. Suddenly much nicer. Perhaps the idea of hanging up on an interested party—any interested party—is losing its appeal.

I hang up, wondering who pays the cell phone bills and who is making a doc about Mitch "Blood" Green.

PROFESSIONAL BOXING ravages the body. I used to be a boxing apologist, explaining to any who would listen that if one quit at the right time and practiced moderation in sparring, etc., that there would be no ill effects. This, I'm learning in the writing of this book, is naive. I've spoken with a handful of men, all of whom have been compromised mentally by boxing. I am not a physician nor have I read the most recent studies. The Joe Mesi situation (a popular heavyweight contender who had his boxing license revoked after it was discovered that he had bleeding on the brain after a recent fight) was a significant media event only because it happened to a white fighter. But I can recognize the symptoms—slurred speech, slow reflexes. When I started the book, I thought that these might be isolated cases limited to a few fighters. But the damage wrought by Tyson and years of boxing is comprehensive and long lasting. Green's case is, perhaps, the most depressing. The fact that he can still be licensed to fight—as he did a month ago in Memphis—is a disservice to the fighter and the sport.

I am sitting in a hotel room in Queens, NY, thinking of all the reasons why I shouldn't call Mitch

Green. The unintelligible messages he has been leaving on my cell phone . . . the fact that he lives in Jamaica, Queens, and has been linked to gangs his entire life. The jail time. The held-up gas stations. The 54 times he's had his driver's license revoked (I can't imagine having to make 54 trips to the bureau of motor vehicles—no wonder he's angry). This, even for a tough-acting boxing writer, is out of my league. It is, after all, mostly an act. I am still feeling sheepish about asking the girl at the front desk to call me a cab just moments after she gave me a free Metro card.

I dial the number. Often when you dial someone hoping to get voicemail, you know they probably won't pick up. Green always picks up.

"Mitch, it's Ted Kluck with the *Facing Tyson* project."

Silence.

"Listen, I'm in Queens for a few more hours and wondered if we might be able to get together."

More silence. Finally, he speaks.

"Where you at?"

I give him my location—a hotel just across the river from Manhattan off the Long Island Expressway. It is next to nothing. Just factories and gas stations. I couldn't even suggest a coffee shop, but Blood Green really isn't the coffee shop type anyway. I imagine us in the hotel lobby, a mental picture that doesn't really take.

"I'm in Jamaica," he replies. My friends told me about Jamaica—told me to steer clear. I ask Green if he could possibly drive up to meet me.

"I don't drive," he says. I am completely unsurprised by this news. He tells me I need to speak with his manager in California before he will agree to any interview. He tells me to call the manager immediately, regardless of the fact that it is 6 A.M. in California. I decide to shift gears.

"Mitch, tell me about your experiences with Don King."

"Don King. Shit. You should call him Don Queen."

"Did King make it tough for you to get fights, after Tyson?" I ask.

"It's Don Queen," he says, correcting me very matter of factly, like a teacher might address a grammar student.

"Right. Don Queen."

We continue on in this vein for several minutes until I can think of nothing more to ask. He is at times belligerent and at times agreeable. Somebody gets called a faggot, although I'm not sure if it's me, the manager, Tyson, or Don King. With Green's diction, combined with two cell phones, we both get almost nothing out of the conversation. I agree to call his manager, despite the early hour. I call him and he sounds alarmingly normal on his voicemail. In fact it is his wife's voice. I immediately feel bad for waking them up. They probably laze out of bed on a Saturday . . . maybe bring back some bagels and read the paper together. She probably wishes he'd give up the boxing thing already. Grow up. Start thinking about the career and the kids. Mitch Green is the last thing she wants to hear about on Saturday morning, I'm pretty sure of that.

CHAPTER FOUR

MARVIS **FRAZIER**

Have I not commanded you? Be strong and courageous. Do not be terrified; do not be discouraged, for the LORD your God will be with you wherever you go.

—JOSHUA 1:9

IT'S RAINING ON Broad Street, and Joe Frazier is considering not letting me inside his gym. I'm here to interview his son Marvis, I tell him, I set it up with Marvis last week. Joe's words are barely discernible—chalk it up to ring wars, age, and a bad cell phone connection. I give my cabbie the universal sign for "stay put for a minute." I'm also having a difficult time communicating with him, and, for a moment, consider giving up on communicating with anyone in Philadelphia. The cabbie, sensing the plight of a white guy in a bad neighborhood, plus the big score of a double-fare, offers to take me back to the airport, which I seriously consider for a moment.

"You need to speak with the PR guy," says Joe Frazier, in a gravely voice. What PR guy? I didn't know there was a PR guy. This is a new development. I quickly add up the cost of the plane ticket, plus cab fare—all for an interview that looks like it's not materializing.

"Can I just come inside and work out the details in there?"

"Not if you haven't talked to the PR guy. If you don't follow the rules, I can't let you in. Hold on." If I were in a movie, talking on a pay phone, this is where I would slam it against the side of the phone booth 15 times. Entering Joe Frazier's gym is proving more difficult than entering the Pentagon.

There is silence on the line while voices can be heard in the background. The neighborhood is a hodgepodge of nail parlors, custom hubcap joints, and the like. It seems an odd place for a cultural icon of Frazier's status. The façade on the front of the gym is so faded that the cabbie and I drove by it the first time. Another voice comes on the line. This one I can understand. It is the PR guy, and I can tell that he feels sheepish about the whole thing. I think he even says so. Go on in, he says. It's no problem as long as you set it up with Marvis ahead of time.

I enter a gym with a ring in the center of the room, bathed in the light of bare light bulbs hanging randomly off the ceiling. My hands are trembling a little bit from the cell phone incident—I hope nobody here notices. Several old, 70s vintage sofas rest in the front area, along with tires, an old motorcycle, and an old pop machine—it could be a frat guy's attic, save for the distinctive smell of "boxing gym."

Big black-and-white photos of Joe Frazier line the walls, along with a large mural of the Frazier family, and the requisite assortment of gloves, bags, and fight posters. There are no pictures of Muhammad Ali, save for an old Ali/Frazier poster tucked into a corner. This is Joe's space, and all the walls are lined with posters containing his words of wisdom: "Get Down or Lay Down." "Respect God, Respect Parents, Respect Brothers and Sisters, Respect Others, Respect Self." Respect journalists who have flown 500 miles to be here was oddly absent. Everything in here is old. Stepping into Joe Frazier's gym is like stepping into the early 1970s—the era in which everybody was making money and all was right with the Frazier family.

I can feel Joe staring down at me, disdainfully, from some remote portion of the gym, pissed that I didn't call the PR guy first. Above the peeling paint and the old equipment is a window—one would assume, his office. I think it's unfortunate that all boxing gyms now look like movie sets. The lockers are old and falling apart, the toilets drip. If I trained here, Frazier would bag my stuff and hang it on a nail, just like they did to Rocky. I should have called the PR guy.

Marvis Frazier greets me with warmth and bright eyes and explains that we can chat as soon as he finishes training his fighters. He is longer of limb than his father, but he still has the thick hips and ass from whence comes the Frazier power. He is dressed in black slacks and a T-shirt—suggesting the balance between his work with fighters and his work running the family foundation. Marvis is 45 years old, but still moves around the gym like a kid—yelling, imploring, spitting, and working his charges on the punch mitts. His Afro is still jet black, save for a streak of white running right down the middle.

A young black boy peppers the heavy bag with quick jabs and hooks in a corner; he can't be more than nine years old but looks like he was born in a boxing gym. The motions are fluid and confident. (His name is Joshua, he's 12, and his record is 3–2.) After working him on the mitts, Frazier turns his attention to an older Asian man who is trying hard, but clearly has no idea what he's doing.

Frazier works with him as enthusiastically as he would train a world champion.

"The jab is your 'search,' the right is 'destroy,'" he says, as the man slaps feebly at his mitts.

"C'mon now," Frazier implores, "nasty, nasty!" The Asian man laughs with delight as he completes a combination. "Make him miss by inches," says Frazier, while teaching slips. Even in a novice, I recognize the Frazier teachings—he has the slightly bent-forward carriage that the elder Frazier used with such effectiveness. Frazier is teaching him to roll with punches and then come back with a right hand/left hook combo. The man, slowly, learns the movements. This, I think, is the charm of boxing. It's a place for misfits, for athletes who would fit in nowhere else. Give us your poor, your tired, your huddled masses. The man drops his hands, exhausted, after the beep of the bell. Life happens at three-minute intervals in the gym.

"SMOKIN' JOE FRAZIER!" bellows Marvis in a perfect imitation of Howard Cosell.

Joe navigates the rickety stairs wearing a pair of linen slacks, a linen shirt, and a nice hat, looking like a black Jay Gatsby. This Frazier was the first US heavyweight boxer in history to win an Olympic gold medal, during the 1964 games in Tokyo. A former world champion, he was immortalized in three legendary bouts with Muhammad Ali. Frazier amassed a 32–4–1 record as a pro, with 27 wins by knockout. Today, though, I fear that he will simply be the guy throwing me out of his gym. He stops to greet Joshua and the Asian fighter, who he says he likes, because he gets to the gym on time.

He finally makes his way to me, extending his hand and smiling, the morning's transgressions all but forgotten. I thank him for having me in his gym and breathe a huge internal sigh of relief. I may actually get this interview.

"I'm outta here," father hollers to son.

"I love you pop."

"BOXING TELLS YOU WHO the real deal is," says Marvis Frazier. "It tells you who's the winner and who's the loser. It builds self-esteem, it builds character. It helps you believe in yourself. I enjoy the camaraderie and the athletes. I have a lot of kids who come in here and are totally introverted . . . but then they get exposed to the camaraderie and start learning the sport, and they come out of their shell. But it's real . . . everybody's not going to be a winner. It parallels life—in life you have to keep your head up and your eyes on the man. You still have the hooks and crooks, the bad guys. You don't like to see when guys train hard and do enough to win the fight but don't get the decision. I don't like that, and I've never liked that about the sport. But that's life, and life is not fair.

"The thing that really bothers me is that you spend a lot of time building fighters . . . guys who at one time didn't know how to wrap their hands or tie their shoes, but then when they think they've made it, they pull down their trunks and say 'kiss this.' But that's life in boxing and you have to live with it. There's just no integrity, no morality. It stems from our society—'it's about me!' We live in a selfish world."

I ask Frazier about Muhammad Ali's role, if any, in shaping the selfish athletic culture we live with today.

"I think he was a prince of showing people in America that we could be what God made us . . . some of the things I agreed with him and some I did not, but he's his own man and he made his own choices about how he would live his life," he says. "One thing you can never take away from him was that he was a great champion in the boxing ring. I'm biased though, people say 'Ali was the greatest guy,' but I say Joe Frazier was the greatest. But you can't say one name without the other . . . there were two dynamics. Ali was the brash, supposedly white-collar, sophisticated Hollywood guy, whereas my father was the farm guy. Then you had the guys who agreed with the war and the guys that disagreed with the war. It created a polarization in our society. It was one of those things where you remember what you were doing . . . when Kennedy got assassinated, when Dr. King got assassinated . . . and when Ali fought Frazier."

We are chatting on the steps leading up to the ring; sitting with the gloves, wraps, and mitts that make up the unchanging mise-en-scène of a boxing gym. Frazier has been around this his whole life. He was the National Golden Gloves heavyweight champion in 1979 and the AAU heavyweight champ in 1980—the year we decided to boycott the Olympic Games in Moscow. Sport giveth and sport taketh away. Frazier, a boxer, not a puncher, was widely considered the nation's best amateur heavyweight, until suffering a one-punch, one-round loss to James Broad. The punch, it turns out, pinched a nerve in Frazier's neck, and instead of starting his professional career with a clean bill of health, he began by rehabbing from corrective surgery. The scar, which runs up the back of his neck, looks not unlike a zipper and is a visible reminder of the sport's physical toll.

Growing up a Frazier had its ups and downs, he says. "I never lacked for anything materially—clothes, GI Joes, shoes—you name it and I could have it. But it was difficult. Everybody wanted to knock you down because you were Joe Frazier's kid. But I'm proud of my dad, and proud of my family."

To say that Frazier is "deeply religious" would be a disservice—writers are always saying that people are "deeply religious," with various levels of sincerity.

However, Christ seems to infuse everything that Frazier does and says. There is an animation to his speech and a light in his eyes when he talks about redemption.

"I became a Christian through my sister Jacqui. Jacqui was on fire for Christ and she kept telling me 'you gotta quit chasing around all these girls or you're gonna burn in Hell!' From time to time she brought some of her Christian girlfriends over to the house, and one day she brought this beautiful young lady, her name was Daralyn, to the house. I said, 'So when we going out?' She said, 'The only way I'll go out with you is if you go to church with me.' I was like 'what?' But little did I know that while I was chasing this girl, Christ was chasing me. I accepted the Lord at age 16 through an altar call. Daralyn became my wife. I've spent the last 14 years of my life trying to tell brothers and sisters about Christ. It's a constant process of giving up control of my life to Him, because before I was living by the James Brown doctrine. You know what that is, right?"

I don't.

"I just got to get up and do my thang!" says Frazier. "Basically a self-centered way of living life. But God came so that we might have life and have it abundantly. But God wants control of our lives, and when we repent it has to cost us something. What it costs us is control.

"I lost my wife four years ago to colon cancer. It was a lot of pain, but that's a part of life. It was hard, but God says he'll never leave me or forsake me and that many are the afflictions of the righteous, but God delivers us out of them all. Trust the Lord with all your heart, lean not on your own understanding. Romans 8:28 says that all things work together for them that are called according to His purpose."

I ask him how he reconciled his faith with such a violent sport.

"If God can use a rooster to speak to Peter, He can use me to do anything. He says in Matthew 5:13 that we are the light of the world, the salt of the earth, but if the salt has lost its saltiness how can it be salt? At that point it's good for nothing but to be trampled by men . . . And he says to let that light, the light of Christ, shine among men. It's how I walk, how I talk, how I live, and how I conduct myself as a man.

"I knew what I was getting into in boxing. We're all warriors. We all know the rules of the game. My dad used to say that in boxing you can get your brains shook, your money took, and your name in the undertaker's book. But the Lord says that he will never leave us or forsake us and that no weapons formed against us shall prosper.

"So many people look at boxing as a brutal sport, but I look at it as competition, as being competitive. I still have all my teeth, and all my faculties. The only way that you'll come out in one piece is if you live by the rules of the game. It starts to tell on you when you hit your 40s, 50s, and 60s, and then you'll tell who was cheatin' and who wasn't. Some guys stay past their prime. You have to know when to get in and when to get out."

Frazier retired from boxing in 1988 after a relatively short pro career, compiling a 19–2 (8 by KO) record. I remark on his relatively short career.

"I had a 56–2 record in the amateurs and beat Tony Tubbs, who became champion, and Tim Witherspoon in the amateurs, and James "Bonecrusher" Smith in the pros—and they all held the title at one time or another," says Frazier, his competitive fires burning. "I beat Smith in the amateurs and the pros. David Bey I beat in the amateurs, but if it was meant to be for me to be champion, if it was God's will, I would have been there. But all anyone remembers is Holmes and Tyson."

Frazier lost only two fights as a pro—to Larry Holmes and Tyson, and it could be argued that he was overmatched in both fights by a father who may have wanted to live out the rest of his boxing dreams through his son. Frazier was confident but inexperienced going into the Holmes fight, and after dancing and taunting was caught with a Holmes right and trapped in the corner, never to return. Mills Lane waived off the bout with 2:57 remaining in the first round.

"As a manager, Joe couldn't help but want to live through his son," says Philadelphia boxing historian John DiSanto. "Marvis was a good fighter, but he just didn't have the tools to stay with Tyson. But I'm sure he went in there to erase his only loss, to Holmes, and I'm sure he thought he could win. I'm not sure what the dollars were, but they were probably offered a big payday, and the fight was on *Wide World of Sports*."

There were many in boxing who also felt that Marvis Frazier should have done his fighting as a cruiserweight.

"Judging by his physique, he appears more suited to the cruisers," said "the fight doctor" Ferdie Pacheco in a 1985 *Ring Magazine* interview. "But the current crop of heavyweights isn't exactly filling anyone with awe. Marvis is never going to be another Joe Frazier, but he should be able to have a good career and earn some bucks. A lot of people wanted Marvis to quit after his loss to Holmes, but don't forget, he was in with one of today's greats and was still on his feet when they stopped it."

"The enduring image I have of Marvis Frazier," says DiSanto "was after his fight with Holmes, after being beaten badly. I remember his dad holding his head and talking to Marvis. It seemed very gentle, almost like Joe was publicly apologizing, or taking the blame, for putting him in with Holmes."

I ask Frazier if his father, who also served as his trainer, felt conflicted sending him in against a 24–0 Mike Tyson who, at the time, was destroying everything in his path.

"Bring on Mike Tyson! I think I could take him now!" he shouts. "That was my attitude. We're warriors. I'm a Frazier! My father knew going in what Mike could do, but we had confidence in my abilities. It's all about faith, and if you don't have faith that you can beat the guy, what are you doing in the ring? I didn't know a thing about Mike at that time except that he was an obstacle on my path to a title, . . . but I guess God had other plans for me! What did I last, 32 seconds?"

Something like that. Frazier is willing to laugh about it, which puts me at ease. Tyson seemed to lift

Frazier off the canvas with a brutal uppercut that ended the fight before it really began, on July 26, 1986, at the Civic Center in Glenns Falls, NY. The fight itself was almost gothically cinematic—the ring situated in the middle of a dark room, bathed in light. The new bull, Tyson, taking on the progeny of the old warrior in Marvis Frazier. This was supposed to be a test for Tyson—a real step up in competition; however, he overwhelmed young Frazier with his speed and power. The fight lasted only 30 seconds and represents the fastest knockout on Mike Tyson's resume. Indeed, Tyson is more like Marvis Frazier's father, Joe Frazier, than Marvis himself. Tyson emulated the elder Frazier's bobbing, weaving, and hooking, often with deadly results.

"It was the speed more than the power," he says. "It's the speed that kills you . . . the punches you don't see are the ones that get you. I didn't even see the uppercut coming."

On film, Tyson can be seen yelling maniacally after the knockout—high on the sweet narcotic of being young, rich, and able to do the thing you love most, better than anyone in the world. Minutes later, in the post-fight interview, he is calm, collected, and articulate. This was an impeccably managed Mike Tyson.

"I knew I was going to stop him in the first round," said an excited Tyson after the fight. He mentioned his trainer Kevin Rooney repeatedly and credited him for installing the uppercut that destroyed Frazier.

"I wrote Tyson a poem when he was in prison," says Frazier. "I didn't know him before we fought and I hadn't really talked to him since, but I just wanted to encourage him and let him know that I was thinking about him. I wanted to show solidarity. As men, in our culture, we dissimilate ourselves every day. We dissemble. It's all about standing out. About saying 'I'm big' or 'I'm tough' or 'I make a lot of money.' It's considered weak to cry. But that's crazy— Christ cried. I think we're called to be pallbearers for each other. It's kind of a morbid term, it's a guy, a brother or a friend, who carries you down to the grave—"

But it means bearing each other's burdens.

"Right. It's because of what happens in our society—kids who grow up without the double L's, love and leadership. God didn't intend for the women just to raise the children, he intended for the family. The glory of children is their fathers. God intended families to have mothers *and* fathers. The majority of men incarcerated today are there because they don't have fathers, the dad wasn't there. It takes a man to raise a man."

Do you have kids?

"I have two daughters and a grandbaby."

He spells their names for me. Tamyra. Tiara. Ki Leah. Our talk turns to prisons and Frazier's work with a ministry called Prison Fellowship, run by former Nixon-aide-turned-white-collar-criminal-turned-evangelist Chuck Colson. It is a ministry that has touched millions, and it sends Frazier in and out of our nation's prisons on a regular basis.

"I wrote Mike a poem when he was incarcerated . . . called 'The Young Man.'" Frazier begins to recite the poem from memory.

"Many years ago they brought us all here by ships. They separated us from our mommas and daddies, they beat us with whips. We became defeated, we almost lost our minds, but a still small voice said, 'Young man, it's prayin time.' I dropped to my knees and cried, 'Man, what have I done?' 'Be still young man, you're a chosen one.' I said, 'Lord, this cup is much much too hard for me to bear, why was I not called to be another man instead?' He said, 'Hold it young man and let me tell you what will become of you if you continue trusting me and to your own self be true. Out of your loins will come prophets, priests, rulers, and kings, so yes young man I expect much from you, especially when they mock and laugh and spit at you too. They will mock you, they will slap you, they will beat you to the ground. But young man, when this world seems to have gotten the best of you, open your Bible, yes, I'm in there, you see, I'm a young man too.'"

Did he respond? Frazier tells me that he responded the day that he was up for parole and they turned him down. Tyson heard that Frazier was out in the yard with Colson, as the two were there for a Prison Fellowship presentation. The two men prayed together, and Tyson thanked him for the letter.

"Mike heard I was out in the yard, he said, 'Man, I got your letter,' and I said a little prayer with him there," says Frazier. "Now whenever he sees me, he bows and compliments me on my family and everything."

"I felt bad for him after his last fight, I really did," says Frazier. "But I feel like God is doing a tremendous work in him, and is going to work through him. God allows us to make our own choices, and He says choose you this day who you'll serve. But the only way a man can come to Christ is if God draws him.

"I love you, Mike, I love you, man. No matter where you are or how you're living right now, God still loves you and I still love you. If there's anything I can do now to get you closer to the Lord and to live a good life and be happy, and to reveal what God can do with you and through you and for you, just let me know."

WE ARE IN HIS OFFICE NOW, and Marvis is playing the blues harp, a beautiful rendition of "Amazing Grace." He has assembled a folder for me to take, including his business card, a glossy photograph, and a 45-rpm record album of his father singing "My Way," the song that made Frank Sinatra famous. The paper cover has yellowed considerably with age. Weirdly, I can't wait to listen to this item that clearly belongs in the so-bad-it's-good category of pop-culture ephemera.

The office is filled with much memorabilia—trophies, plaques, and a giant *Life* magazine cover depicting Ali and Frazier standing next to one another. And a bespectacled Marvis Frazier is sitting behind his computer ("I'm just getting comfortable with e-mail," he says). On his desk is a stack of business books—topics ranging from the motivational to the spiritual. Frazier is currently in charge of running a family nonprofit, of which the gym is a part.

The gym door opens and a tough-looking young guy walks in—hat at an angle, Jhericurl, NBA jacket. He looks nervous. Walking into a boxing gym for the first time takes the swagger out of any man.

"Is anyone here?" he asks. He has come to get an application, to start boxing. Marvis fills him in on the basics—$100 bucks to join; $50 a month gets you a locker and use of the gloves and headgear in the gym. Everything else you provide. The guy is 26 and has never boxed before. Says he's done some scrapping on the street (girlfriend rolls eyes), but that he wants to get into boxing for the stress relief and self-esteem. He really said self-esteem. This makes me smile. Marvis shakes his hand and we all make our way toward the door.

"What's your name, sir?" the man asks Frazier as we exit the gym.

"Marvis," he replies, his last name conspicuous only in its absence.

CHAPTER FIVE

JOSE **RIBALTA**

Heroes and cowards feel exactly the same fear.
Heroes just react to it differently.

—CUS D'AMATO

THE CORNERS ALL LOOKED the same. At whatever
point a guy realized he could hang with Mike Tyson,
the corner between rounds took on the appearance of
a New Year's Eve celebration—full of hope, activity,
and excitement. Tyson's corners, by contrast, were
run like staff meetings—Kevin Rooney presenting
minutes about the tasks at hand and Tyson, barely
breathing heavily, taking it all in.

Jose Ribalta was the only one in his corner that
didn't look scared at the Trump Plaza on August 17,
1986. A tall, dark fighter of Cuban birth, Ribalta
stood six feet six inches and had to work to look
down to meet Tyson's eyes during the pre-fight staredown. He should have been scared, but wasn't, which
in retrospect must have been a little disconcerting for
a Tyson who had in the span of eight previous weeks

mowed down Reggie Gross (TKO 1), William Hosea
(KO 1), Lorenzo Boyd (KO 2), and Marvis Frazier
(KO 1). Ribalta simply, as remembered by Tyson aide
Steve Lott, "came to fight."

Ribalta was all arms and legs and boasted an 81-
inch reach—however, his strategy wasn't to run and
jab but rather, like Kevin McBride would years later,
frustrate Tyson by hooking Tyson's arms and then
punching in combinations. Ribalta moved about the
ring like a man doing a job, as opposed to a man on
professional death row, as per so many Tyson opponents. He also had the audacity to bounce up, after
Tyson caught him with a hellacious uppercut that
snapped his head backward and lifted him up off the
canvas in round two. Ribalta then managed to stay
off the canvas until round 8 by punching in combinations and managing to awkwardly but effectively tie
Tyson up. And in spite of Tyson's star status, the
crowd could even be heard chanting Ribalta's name
on occasion.

A rugged pro at 23–3, Ribalta had been in against
big names before and is almost universally thought to
have been jobbed on a split decision loss to James
"Bonecrusher" Smith in a fight where he overcame a
1st-round knockdown to regain control. Ribalta's
professionalism was evident in his ability to stick to
the fight plan, even after the knockdown. And as he
did so, Tyson became frustrated and began to headhunt. Ribalta continued to punch and clutch—not
winning rounds so much as proving that he belonged,
and that Tyson may not be the knockout machine
that he was billed. But Tyson was hungry and well

conditioned, and, as such, would eat. He blasted Ribalta's mouthpiece into the nether regions of the casino in round 8, and later had Ribalta down again in the 8th. The crowd, however, had begun to show its appreciation to Ribalta. After an early knockdown in round 10, Ribalta answered in the affirmative and continued fighting bravely. After another knockdown in round 10, the referee stepped in to rescue a wounded Ribalta on the ropes.

Tyson's postfight reaction was atypical for him at the time. Usually he was quick to console the other fighter with an embrace, a word of encouragement, and handshakes in the opposing corner. This time he simply walked to his side of the ring—perplexed, perhaps, to have had to work so long to get Ribalta out of there. Tyson landed an efficient 68 percent of his punches and controlled throughout, but the fighter and his public both, by this time, demanded explosive knockouts. Ribalta, for his part, may have engendered more respect from the boxing community in this defeat than he had in any of his previous 22 victories.

"Mike knew that Cus expected him to be exciting—and he knew that he just had to get in there and wing shots in the direction of the other guy," said Lott. "Mike knew what to say to the media in regards to what he thought he should be able to do against certain guys—but in private he would admit, and Cus would have said, that he should have been able to get this guy out of there in a couple of rounds.

"We didn't know much about Ribalta going in. We saw him fight on video, but when he got into the ring, he raised his level of performance by about 18 levels, which made for a spectacular fight. The first couple of rounds were a war."

SOUTH BEACH, IN MIAMI, is a whole pseudo-city of Paris Hilton look-alikes—emaciated blondes with rich, cappucino tans, too much makeup, and big, fake breasts. Techno music tinkles out of storefronts, where in one stop you can grab a pair of guido-fabulous Gucci-knockoff loafers, a laptop computer, and a slice of cheap pizza. It is an area where everyone acts like everyone else is looking at them, and they're probably not wrong in thinking that. As such, I have an almost obsessive desire to find the other normal couple here and ask them to dinner. I see a man wearing white tennis shoes with jeans, his wife is wearing the Midwestern Mom high-waisted jean shorts with a camera slung over her shoulder. They look like schoolteachers. Probably social studies or math. I wonder if they want to hang out.

In spite of his surroundings, Jose Ribalta is the antithesis of self-possessed. He is a giant man (six feet six inches) with a friendly face and wire-rimmed glasses, who, aside from the occasional flecks of gray on his shaved head, could pass for much younger. His shoulders have the requisite huge slope of the athlete, and I learn that before a run-in with a high school coach, he was drawing the interest of NCAA football recruiters from Miami, Purdue, and several other schools. Ribalta's first dream was to be a college football player.

"My coach shoved me one day in practice coming back to the huddle," he says, quietly, in a voice that is close to a whisper. "I punched him. The coach told the team that I had made a different choice for my career . . . that I had chosen boxing. He said, 'How can I let you back on the team after you do something like that?' He lied to them, basically. I was jayvee all-city, and then I made the varsity. I loved football."

He pauses, a looks to his lawyer and friend, Jeff Cummins, who has joined us for the interview.

"Jeff, I'm kind of nervous."

Jeff Cummins has offered his office as a meeting place on his day off. He is dressed in skeet-shooting clothes and is himself a former fighter. After speaking with him on the phone, I expected him to be a large man with a mustache; he is, rather, a small man with a mustache and a large man's voice. He cares about Ribalta, has known him since Jose was this tall (makes childhood height with arm). Covering boxing has taught me that the fighters that turn out okay in life are largely surrounded by people like Cummins— people who care but are not trying to make their livelihood off the fighter. Still, Cummins strikes me as the kind of lawyer who, if you crossed him, would probably rip your still-beating heart out of your chest and feed it to you.

"I was a high school wrestler, but I didn't have much in the way of moves," Cummins recalls. "And this is about as big as I get . . . about 175. I couldn't beat the real 175 guys, so I fought heavyweight and I lost in the quarterfinals to a guy from Seneca, New York, who weighed 405 pounds. People thought he was going to sit on me and crush me. So one day my dad, who fought, told me that I would probably be a better puncher than a grappler, since I was coordinated and could hit a baseball. Can you imagine a father encouraging his son to get into boxing? (I can't.) So I picked it up and boxed some in college at Drew University. After I lost my eigth amateur fight, my trainer encouraged me to get out of it. He said, 'You're going to run out of eye tissue and brain tissue.' I was starting to see spots in the periphery of my vision."

It's astonishing, and a little endearing, that this giant across the table is nervous. He has turned down several requests for interviews to talk about Tyson in books and on Web sites over the years. I ask him to tell me how his family came to the United States.

"We had a big struggle leaving Cuba," he says, relaxing. "One of the big reasons we came over was Castro. My father worked for the president of Cuba, Batista, and couldn't leave the country . . . he was accused of shooting a guy and they were trying to kill him. Castro was in power then and was looking to kill all of Batista's people [Fulgencio Batista overthrew brutal dictator Gerardo Machado in 1933, and after another coup in 1952 became Cuba's president, only to run his own oppresive and corrupt regime and be overthrown by Fidel Castro fighting with Che Guevara—he of the college town T-shirts—in 1959]. But my family was pretty well off, so my father sent my mother and the younger kids to the US. My oldest brother had already turned 16, and it was mandatory that at 16 you have to do some time in the military, so my mother said she loved Cuba and didn't want to leave. But my father said, 'You don't want to sacrifice one child to save the others?'"

"Jose, tell him your brothers' names," adds Cummins. "How many of them were named Jose?"

"My brothers and I were all named Jose," he says. "We did it before George Foreman. I think he learned it from us. You're from a different culture so it's hard for you to understand . . . but my mother believed in Santoria. I remember when my father was lying in the hospital, this woman came in and said, 'If I walk around the room one time, he'll die.' But she made it halfway around the room and fell down."

In spite of those challenges, Ribalta grew up in a house that was "big and happy," remembers Cummins. "It was a big house—I wouldn't have minded growing up in that house—but there were always people everywhere. You might have to sleep on the patio."

The Ribaltas spent nearly two years in Washington, DC, where Jose's mother stayed home to look after the children and Jose was navigating the unique social challenges that come with being a schoolkid in an American city.

"The dark-skinned American kids in DC made fun of us," he says. "People would pick at us. They would pick at me. But finally I stood up to them and said if you want something from me, you're going to have to be able to take it. They didn't understand the way we talked, but then we moved to Miami and it got better."

Miami was also where Ribalta found boxing, after following his brother Augustine (a pro with an 11–1 record at the time) to the Moore Park gym in Miami.

"My mom told me I couldn't box at first," he recalls, "but one day I started following him to the gym."

"Bobby Allen, right?" asks Cummins. Allen was the proprietor of the gym and is something of a fixture in South Florida boxing.

"I kept talking to my oldest brother in Cuba, who had lost a couple of really close decisions to Teofilo Stevenson. I fought in the amateurs and lost in the finals of the National Golden Gloves to a guy named Johnny Williams, who is dead now . . . got shot over a young lady."

Ribalta's father passed away in 1984, as a result of gunshot wounds he sustained during the conflicts in Cuba. However, he was able to spend the last five years of his life in the United States and was able to see Jose fight professionally.

Ribalta says this with an amazing matter-of-factness. Indeed, the conversation often shifts to who is living and who is dead, a catching-up process between Ribalta and his lawyer. Ribalta's cell phone chirps periodically, and he pauses to answer, smiling often. Jose Ribalta is a friend to fighters. He chats up old cruiserweight Uriah Grant. Calls Chico from Warriors Boxing to get me a phone number—"I've got a friend here, a book writer, needs a couple of numbers." Chico is screaming at someone in the gym, in Spanish, embroiled in an argument such that Ribalta pulls the nearly jumping phone away from his ear and clicks it shut, says he'll call back later.

He turned pro in 1982 and fought often—ten times in 1982, all wins, until a setback at the hands of Ricardo Richardson in 1983. Ribalta's only losses before the Tyson fight were to James "Bonecrusher" Smith (a fight some thought he won) and Marvis Frazier. Both fights went the distance. Ribalta's activity in the early years was both a function of his skill and hungry, sometimes unscrupulous, management.

"Jose was a creature of bad management, which you see a lot in boxing. He had no money for training," says Cummins, clearly annoyed by the decisions of his early management. "He did not have a manager who would spend money on him, whereas Tyson's people were bringing in the best sparring partners for him. If Jose wanted to lift weights, he had to go to a public gym. I never saw him get a rubdown, and Tyson, training at Gleasons or wherever he trained, had rubdowns and weight lifting whenever he wanted it."

According to Ribalta, he was owed several thousand dollars for training expenses before the Tyson fight, which he never saw ("Make sure you put that in there," he insists). Instead of sparring with top heavyweights to prepare him for Tyson, he ended up sparring with cruiserweight Carlos De Leon, who hurt him with a left hook in sparring just a few days before the fight. Ribalta, battling the flu, also lost 11 pounds in the three days before the bout.

"It's a major regret," says Cummins. "I was sort of friends with Jim Jacobs—he's gone now, do you know who he is? He was a boxing historian and was involved with a few fights. I called up because Jose's then manager was not really a man of letters—nor was he licensed to do anything but manage fighters. I made the initial calls to Jacobs—and tried to get him what I thought he deserved, which was about $200,000. I tried to do that and I started negotiating, but then his manager said 'I'd better take it from here,' so what he got him was not $200,000, but what he got him was $52,000. Can you imagine fighting Mike Tyson for $52,000?"

It has also been discussed that perhaps Ribalta took the Tyson fight before he was really ready to face a fighter of his caliber.

"If he'd waited, if he'd waited for Tyson to knock out two more guys, he might have gotten $200,000 . . . he might have gotten a million!"

"My trainer, Dave Clark, was always nervous with me. He treated me like a father and took care of me," says Ribalta. "He always thought that I was a year or two away from being ready to fight Tyson, just maturity-wise. To a degree I agree with him."

I remark that as opposed to Tyson's other opponents, Ribalta seemed to show no fear as he walked into the ring with Tyson, and as the fight progressed.

"I was nervous but I was not afraid of him," he recalls. "I usually regurgitated once before every fight . . . and I regurgitated twice before Tyson. I said to myself, 'Man, this is a mean guy, I gotta put my pants on the right way. But then when I saw him smiling in the ring after he beat Marvis Frazier, I said, 'This guy is a sissy.' And then I saw him in the hotel before the fight. He was standing next to an elevator talking to a young lady and I looked over at him and raised my fist and said, 'I'm going to knock your a-s-s out.'"

Ribalta spells "ass," too polite to actually use the word in this context.

"Tyson looked back at me," he continues, "and he just smiled. That's when I knew I was going to be in for a hard fight."

Ribalta was right, and he was the victim of a nasty Tyson uppercut in the second round that left him on the canvas. He got up, however, and continued to fight.

"He didn't really hurt me with that punch," he says. "I was more off balance than anything. But Tyson was so strong. It's like his legs were stuck in the ground. He was fast and he hit you with combinations . . . it was more than just a one-punch thing with Tyson. As far as one-punch power, I think Bonecrusher Smith hit harder."

"Tyson made people nervous, and nervous is the adult version of crying," says Cummings. "Remember when you were a kid and you just wanted to lay down and take a nap? That's how Tyson made most people feel."

Nobody in the boxing world gave Ribalta a chance, figuring it would be another two-round, clean Tyson execution. Larry Merchant even went so far as to call Ribalta a "knuckleballer" before the fight. But by taking Tyson's best shots and lasting into the 10th round, Ribalta gained respect, and, in spite of the fact that he was ranked as high as number two in the world and fought 11 world champions, he considers his performance against Tyson his greatest achievement.

JOSE RIBALTA'S MOST IMPRESSIVE attribute may in fact be his lack of introspection, which in our culture—

where introspection has become a marketing tool of epic proportions—is saying something. He is unmarried and works security at a local high school for at-risk kids. He has a 12-year-old son from a prior relationship who he would prefer to keep out of boxing. Too many crooks in this sport, he says, impassively and without anger. He wishes he had made more money on the Tyson fight. He thinks Mike Tyson is a good man, and hopes he (Tyson) can stay out of trouble. He sees this interview not as an opportunity to reminisce and feel feel famous again, but rather as a chance to right past wrongs.

"I was brought in to spar with Tyson in 1999," he remembers. "And every day in the gym he would have other guys in the ring and just be knocking them out, one by one. And after he would knock them out, he would glare right at me. He looked very angry. The other fighters would say, 'Man, Ribalta, look at the way Tyson is looking at you.' It turns out he was upset over something a reporter said I said about Tyson being done . . . that he should get out of the fight game. But I want him to know that I never said it."

"I think Tyson would have been much more effective if they'd taught him not to fight out of hatred," says Cummins. "It was like one of those cartoons, watching him in those days. They would just wind him up . . . and if he didn't blast a guy out immediately, he would start to head hunt. You saw it a little bit against Jose."

The subject of Tyson's legacy is discussed.

"I think his impact was mainly positive," says Ribalta. "People look down on him because of his last performaces, but I think he would have beaten Ali in his prime. He was faster and he moved his head more than Joe Frazier. He was 225 pounds and explosive . . . and he was a very hard target to hit."

"Have you talked to anyone about what happened to him, down in Indiana?" asks Cummins, referring to Tyson's three-year imprisonment on rape charges, stemming from an incident with a Miss Black America contestant in an Indianapolis hotel. I reply that I haven't, preferring to keep focused on the fighters and away from anything tabloidish. But as he is a lawyer, I am interested in his professional opinion.

"I never quite understood that case," he says. "How he could go away for three years in a case where there was no physical evidence of wrongdoing? I mean . . . I wouldn't see myself being friends with Tyson . . . I doubt we'd go to ball games or go skeet shooting together, but I still never felt right about that case."

I have tried unsuccessfully to get Ribalta to talk about his legacy, about how he wishes to be remembered. After Tyson, he strung together several victories, only to spend the larger part of the 1990s working as an opponent for those in the heavyweight world class, including Larry Holmes, Tony Tubbs, and Frank Bruno; and later Vitali Klitschko, Chris Byrd, and Razor Ruddock. On the subject of legacy, he will only say that the kids at the school where he works often threaten to knock his a-s-s out. He spells it out, again.

"They say that Tyson knocked me out and that they can knock me out too," he says. I search him for any signs of pain that this may cause him. I keep to myself the idea that there is perhaps nothing worse than being mocked by schoolchildren, and then realize that this is probably why Ribalta fought for a living and I didn't. These things don't really bother him. Kids can be mean, I say. Kids are jerks, adds Cummins. I look for any indication that it bothers him that after an accomplished career, kids only remember him for a loss. I find none.

"I miss boxing," he says. "I miss the physical contact, and the publicity. I used to go out to eat here and people would say 'Jose, your money is no good here.' Now, I'm just a regular guy . . . it's hard to be, like, a common individual now. Every once in a while though, a kid at school will come up to me and say 'Hey man, my dad said you were a helluva fighter.' I like that."

CHAPTER SIX

JAMES "BONECRUSHER" SMITH

Standing on the defensive indicates an insufficience of strength; attacking, a superabundance of strength.

—SUN TZU, *THE ART OF WAR*

MY WIFE THINKS IT'S SILLY that he still uses the handle "Bonecrusher" when he leaves a voicemail at our home. She asks me if I'm going to use a nickname like Ted "The Key Crusher" Kluck when I call him back.

I'm learning that Bonecrusher Smith is many things now, most of which still revolve around him being Bonecrusher Smith, hence the continued use of the name. He slides a business card across his office desk. The card is emblazoned with cruise ships, sunsets, Mount Rushmore, and the like. Bonecrusher Smith is a travel agent. The gist of the business is that when Bonecrusher Smith signs up another "travel agent," that agent gets to travel for discounted rates, and can also sign up other agents under him/her—a cut of which will also go to Bonecrusher Smith. That's how I understand it to work, although I could be wrong.

The office is scantily decorated—in it are just a gray desk, a black chair, and a cubicle-type partition. No pictures of family, and nothing to suggest that he had a boxing career. This is a working space, and the kind of space that looks like it can be quickly vacated if things don't exactly work out.

"Check out Bonecrushertravel.com if you get a chance. You need your own travel Web site, Ted. You might as we'll get paid to travel, right? What do you think?"

Bonecrusher Smith always wants to know what I think, and not in a rhetorical way. He keeps his eyes trained on me in the office as I look up from my notepad.

Bonecrusher Smith is a salesman. He lays out his vision, while sliding a pair of forms—one for sponsorship and one for registration—across the desk.

"What we're doing is a 'Legends of Boxing Cruise,' where I get these fighters together . . . these are tentative commitments . . . [names like Gerry Cooney, Aaron Pryor, Alexis Arguello populate the flyer] and teach them how they can make business opportunities for themselves by leveraging their names in the travel business. These guys were champions, they worked hard, but a lot of them are in rough shape now. I've got over 400 travel agents underneath me. We're doing the cruise April 15, and we're going from Miami to the Grand Caymans to Jamaica. We'll also have a situation where we let the fans be part of a DVD with these guys. I think fans will buy a DVD with these guys—what do you think? I also need somebody to write me up a book real quick—Bonecrusher Smith, first college graduate to win the heavyweight championship—to sell on the cruise as well. And I need to get an artist to do up a flyer like this one [slides a cover of the International Boxing Hall of Fame program across the desk], real slick. What do you think?"

Before he was a travel agent, James "Bonecrusher" Smith was the first college graduate to win the heavyweight title. He has a degree in business from Shaw University in Raleigh, NC. This, the degree, led me to question his pull to boxing in the first place.

"I wanted people to remember me when I died," he says. "I was running out of things to try. I played basketball as a kid . . . I was a runner. I loved running. I didn't know if it was gonna be running the football, running with a basketball, or what. I wanted to be the first at something—when you're first at something that makes you special, it makes you unique."

James Smith was born in 1953 in Magnolia, NC, the son of tobacco farmers.

"My dad just passed in March," he says. "My mom is still alive, and I've got two brothers and three sisters."

His parents, he says, didn't really know what to think about his boxing career—as they would have preferred that he didn't play football, for fear of injuries. He served a stint in the military and after basic training at Fort Jackson in South Carolina was stationed in Germany, Kansas, and New Jersey. Smith's official job function was personnel records, but, as he recalls, "I mostly boxed." I ask Smith what drew him to boxing, his favorite aspect of the sport.

"I liked to travel. And the money. The fans were really good too . . . I liked the fans."

Smith lost his first professional fight on ESPN in November of 1981 against the hard-punching James Broad. He was 28 years old. By November of 1984 he was losing a bid for the IBF heavyweight title to Larry Holmes. Smith's is the odd champion's resume in that it's peppered with losses—17 in total. Before winning the WBA title, Smith lost to Holmes, Tony Tubbs, Tim Witherspoon, and Marvis Frazier—good fighters but far from a murderer's row.

He got his title shot in December of 1986 against Tim Witherspoon, as a last-minute replacement for Tony Tubbs.

"I fought him at Madison Square Garden in New York City," Smith recalls. "I got a call from a certain bushy-haired promoter . . . saying that they needed a replacement and that this was my shot. I had to be ready in one week. I said, 'DK, I'll take it.' I might never get a shot again. I had an early morning negotiation with King . . . I felt like David . . . I mean, I come from a town of 500 people. But I can tell you that I beat both his fighter, Witherspoon, and King in seven days. He had an army of lawyers, but when you're right and you've got the right person on your side, you can beat anyone."

He leans back and folds his arms behind his head, feeling I suppose the same thrill he feels when he signs a new travel client. I ask him to elaborate. I have heard other fighters tell of King's early morning negotiating tactics. King, in fact, was a master of knowing his audience. For some, he knew that briefcases full of cash did the trick. For others, it was late nights in cold rooms, pounding out the particulars of contracts that would send much to King and little to the men doing the work in the ring.

Smith leans back in his chair, laughs, and says he would rather not comment on Don King. Smith is a large man. He stands about six feet four inches, and, like most heavyweights, has huge hands. His countenance now is largely happy and friendly, his face rounded by a few extra post-sport pounds. But like most fight people, Bonecrusher Smith is completely unwilling to discuss Don King. King is that rare adult who can inspire fear in the hearts of other men who normally aren't scared of much. When one thinks of King, one thinks of things like trunks of cars and cement shoes. He is a bad gangster movie come to life.

Smith beat Witherspoon (25–2–0) that evening in New York City—"I had him down three times in the first round"—but his reign would be short-lived. "And the new heavyweight champion of the world . . . " says Smith, reminiscing.

A scant three months later Smith would relinquish the title to Tyson, as part of his quest to unify the heavyweight titles via HBO's heavyweight unification tournament.

"You know I was the first guy to take him twelve rounds," Smith says. He leans back in the office chair to gauge my reaction. The black leather chair groans and seems positively chintzy under his girth. Herman

Miller clearly doesn't design much office furniture for former heavyweight champions.

Many people in and out of boxing thought that Smith had the stature and the punch to take the fight to Tyson. In the press conferences leading up to the fight, Smith, seen prowling the hotel in a cowboy hat, promised a shootout. He was an eloquent champion, as was to be expected from a college graduate. He sounded reasonable and rational speaking in the pre-fight press. He declared himself immune to "Tysoni-tis," the tendency of fighters to become awestruck by Tyson, his mystique, and his entourage. "I plan to win the fight," Smith said then. "He hasn't fought the caliber of guys I have."

This is both true and not true. While Tyson was just beginning his ascent, he had destroyed Trevor Berbick and Marvis Frazier in devastating fashion, so it wasn't so much who he'd beaten at that time, but rather how he had beaten them. The fight was a part of a heavyweight title unification "tournament," hatched with the twofold purpose of providing a slate of saleable heavyweight fights for Don King and HBO, and also providing the public with an undisputed heavyweight champion of the world. A champion who would be required to fight at least two defenses under the Don King banner.

King was, and is, the heavyweight division's power broker, having controlled the major players in the division for the better part of two decades. He has massaged his image now to such an extent that he is a regular guest on the ultraconservative Fox News, waving the American flag and generally playing the role of the common-man-made-good-by-hard-work-and-opportunism. The wolf in patriot's clothing. It was such opportunism that led him out of the corner of a losing George Foreman, whom he had latched onto before his bout in Zaire with Muhammad Ali, and into the corner of Ali, the winning fighter. That walk around the ring, now the stuff of legend, would effectively begin his walk through the heavyweight division. His history is no secret—former Cleveland racketeer, did time, etc. He works a sentence like a fighter works a heavy bag—pounding and manipulating the English language until he reaches the desired effect. He is known for unconventional negotiating techniques—late night phone calls, cold rooms, etc. But, for boxing, none of this is unusual. If boxing's players did things in normal ways, there would be something horribly wrong.

Tyson had already dispatched Trevor Berbick in brutal fashion for the WBC crown. Berbick was a sturdy, if inconsistent, fighter who proved awkwardly effective in wresting the title from Pinklon Thomas.

"Let me tell you a story about the Berbick fight," said former Tyson manger Steve Lott, in a later interview. "The night before the Berbick fight I, like you, wanted to get a feel for Mike's mind-set going in—was he nervous? Was he confident? So I decided to play a little game with him as we were driving back from the video store with some movies. I said, 'Mike, what do you think Cus [D'Amato] would think of this guy [Berbick]?' He thought for a minute and said, 'He'd think he was a tomato can.' That's when I thought to myself 'Oh shit, Berbick's in trouble.'"

Tyson would take care of Berbick in two rounds, utilizing his patented right hook to the body, right uppercut to the chin combination to leave Berbick reeling, drunk, around the ring. Tyson was, officially, the new king of the division. His next challenger was James "Bonecrusher" Smith.

"My game plan was not to be bullied by Mike Tyson," Smith says now. "But Tyson had the aura, and guys he fought got caught up in that aura. It's the circus surrounding Tyson that you get caught up in. Make sense? I was amazed that Larry Holmes, who had that much savvy and experience, had so much trouble with him. Honestly, Mike Weaver, Tim Witherspoon, and Frank Bruno punched harder than he did."

Bonecrusher the salesman pauses for effect. What do you think?

Whatever. I'm not buying.

"I really feel like I could have knocked him out . . . [smacks fist into palm] . . . because I was a big heavyweight."

What Tyson and Smith delivered was far from the promised shootout; rather, it looked more like a high school dance, with Smith clutching and retreating at every opportunity. Tyson would chase Smith around the ring and throw bombs, looking for the spectacular knockout that HBO and the public expected. He began early to headhunt, going away from his usually devastating body attack. Tyson, in fact, lost his cool after the first round, taunting Smith before returning to his corner, where he was chided by trainer Kevin Rooney. The crowd booed lustily. Referee Mills Lane deducted a point from James Smith in the second round for holding. Smith, cut above his left eye in the 3rd round, seemed content to retreat for the duration, often nearly turning his back on Tyson, performing a dainty pirouette that had him turning his shoulder and walking a retreat. It is unknown if the cut or "Tysonitis" was the reason for the retreat, but for whatever reason, the cowboy was shooting blanks.

"People don't understand that Mike in that era was only reaching about 15 to 20 percent of his potential in the ring, compared to what he was doing in the gym," says Lott. "He would get tense and uptight in the ring, especially against better competition. But Mike did things with head movement and combinations in training that defied description. Some fights he relaxed and let it fly . . . like Reggie Gross, and Berbick to some extent, because Berbick was such a stiff. Now Bonecrusher was a little more confident . . . but he didn't initiate, and as a result Mike was hesitant to initiate. The result, unfortunately, was a boring fight."

"I hit him hard in the last round," says Smith of a shot that he landed near the end of the 12th, after being taunted and implored to fight by Tyson. In the fight, Tyson landed 60 percent of his shots to Bonecrusher's 23. He won every round.

"I feel good but I don't feel satisfied," said Tyson in a post-fight interview, Don King hovering over his right shoulder. "He was just out there to survive, but I thought he would come out and try to beat me up."

I ask Bonecrusher Smith the usual question about regrets. He gives me the usual answer about having none, but I let it hang in the air for a minute—that minute in which regrets typically come to the surface.

"I should have come out in that 1st round and jumped on him. I should have let my hands go. I do that and he goes down. Boom. Tyson had trouble with people who weren't bullied and intimidated by him—you saw that with Holyfield and Lennox Lewis later. When you don't get intimidated by him, he's just another small heavyweight . . . but I got a little freaked out by him.

"I wish I would have just knocked him out in the 1st round." He says this again as if it could have happened, like falling out of bed.

Smith's career saw him winning 44 times, losing 17. He fought consistently up through the 1990s, until a 1999 loss to Larry Holmes in something called the "Legends of Boxing" heavyweight tournament put him into retirement for good. The tournament was a hackneyed idea hatched to dust off heavyweights such as Mike Weaver and Tim Witherspoon, along with Holmes and Bonecrusher Smith, to fill a vacant Legends of Boxing heavyweight title—ostensibly giving fans the chance to enjoy their former heroes at a more leisurely pace. A boxing senior circuit.

"You know, that tournament was my idea, my concept. I found an investor down in the Bahamas to put up the money for me to fight Larry Holmes, with the winner to fight George Foreman. The Foreman fight never materialized . . . I don't think he was ever serious. He was just talking. We didn't really have any names to fight with. They just took it and ran with it."

Do you miss the fight game?

"Not at all. It only takes one fight too many for you to end up like these guys [he points to photos of Bobby Chacon and Terry Norris on a Boxing Hall of Fame program], slurring your words and walking on your heels. Once you go over that line, once you take that last shot too many, you can't come back. I'm trying to reach these guys and teach them that there's another way out there to make money. Right? We're going to do at least two cruises, maybe four, and make some money. We can go somewhere every 60 to 90 days to sell books and autographs and make some money. Or they can sell travel like I do and then take these trips and write them off on their taxes because they're in the travel business. They get to have fun and make money. What do you think?"

I would like to have fun and make money, I reply.

"I've got over 400 people in my organization," he adds. "I'm going to Boston tomorrow. You see, whatever I put my name on is going to sell with the positive image. All we've gotta do is put it together. I'm pretty sure Gerry Cooney would want to do a cruise, and maybe Bernard Hopkins. I mean, what's better than living on a cruise ship?"

Not much, I say. It's hard to argue with that pitch. I try to steer the discussion off of travel and on to family. Smith and his wife have been married for 25 years and he has two daughters, both in college, as well as a stepson who is 32. He is intentional about steering them away from a career in the ring.

"Boxing's too tough," he says. "There are easier ways to make a living."

I ask how his wife reconciled his choice of careers.

"She loved to travel too," he says, "and I was the one taking the punches."

Smith's office is housed on the campus of Sandhills Community College in North Carolina. It is a tidy little campus tucked away amidst pine trees and winding roads. Its parking lots are named after great thinkers—Einstein, Faulkner, etc. Smith has a window overlooking a gymnasium where he will eventually teach boxing to the young men at the school. He is trying to encourage young black men to come to the school and is meeting a group there as we walk through the lobby. They address him as Bonecrusher, which makes him smile. It looks to be about 180 degrees outside. You can see the heat wafting up from the parking lot pavement. On the way out he hands me a homemade DVD of his *Greatest Fights and Knockouts* (the DVD is marked with a price tag of $19.99 and contains about 15 minutes of content, which works out to a little over a buck per minute), along with brochures for BonecrusherTravel and his nonprofit, which offers mentoring for wayward youth. He has just started working out again, he says, and explains the parallels between boxing and business.

"You have to believe that you can win in boxing, and you have to believe that you can win in business," he says. I wonder aloud what he would say to Mike Tyson, if he had a few moments alone to mentor him, Smith being a reverend and all.

"It's interesting that you mention that," he replies, pausing for a moment to collect his thoughts. "What's he gonna do now? It's obvious he can't fight anymore if he can't beat a Kevin McBride. What's he going to do, be a missionary?"

Smith chuckles out loud at his own comment, leaning back in the strained Herman Miller. Tyson, in his comments after the McBride fight, intimated at a desire to become a missionary to the Sudan. Smith, ostensibly a man of the cloth himself, is scoffing.

"Of all the people to want to be a missionary," he says. "Kind of ironic, isn't it?"

I ask him how he made his foray into the ministry.

"When I was small, my parents and grandparents took us to church on Sunday . . . talked to us about the Lord, about how He works in people's lives, and the importance of being a good person, and I just kind of continued that," he says. "Now that I'm 52 and I see people leaving this world [dying] . . . I say to myself their spirit has to be going somewhere . . . either heaven or hell. So my ministry is partly to insure that I get to the right place. As I encourage people to be saved and get to the right place, I'm also encouraging myself to get to the right place straight. I'm just reminding myself as I remind others that life is short and eternity is a long time. We don't know when we're going to leave here. We could get up tomorrow and put our shoes on and the undertaker could take them off. You follow?"

I find myself defending Tyson's crude spirituality, his search for meaning and redemption and his desire to help others. I get nowhere. James "Bonecrusher" Smith is laughing out loud at me now.

"The other part [boxing] is gone. He's got to deal with life now . . . he's got to start acting right and doing the right things. He needs a mentor, somebody who's been where he's been . . .

"What do you think?"

Silence.

"Hmm?"

I nod in the affirmative, mainly just to move things along, and suddenly he turns serious. It is time for the close.

"We have a situation here. I need to get ahold of him [Tyson], by the way. Mike Tyson needs to make money now that his boxing career is over. He can't fight anymore. But if he can put 20,000 people in the MCI Center, let's put 15,000 people on the ship and make us a million dollars. Nobody has to get hit in their head . . . you could even come on the ship and sell a few books too. What if he could make money and have some fun at the same time?

"How does that sound?"

CHAPTER SEVEN

PINKLON THOMAS

People, especially if they come up in a rough area, have to go through a number of experiences in life that are intimidating and embarrassing. These experiences form layer after layer over their capabilities and talents. Your job as a teacher is to peel off the layers.

—CUS D'AMATO

PONTIAC, MICHIGAN, is a contradiction of itself. Off Highway 75 between Detroit and Flint, it is both the territory of khaki and golf shirt-clad automotive engineers and a piece of the Detroit ghetto. Where one block houses a Starbucks franchise, the next features an underfunded public school and a section of bombed out housing. These are the streets where my subject used to chase his fix, as early as age eight. This is where I met Pinklon Thomas again for the first time in two years.

I enter the house and find a man on the sofa looking like a very old version of Pinklon himself.

"This is the Bossman," says D. J. Thomas, Pinklon's wife.

I grip the Bossman's bony hand. He is 90 years old. The television in the background is spitting some nonsense about somebody killing somebody; about a car found at the bottom of a lake. Welcome to Detroit.

The home itself is tiny. There is a large tapestry of a very European-looking Christ hanging on one wall, surrounded by shots of Pinklon Thomas in various stages of his boxing career. There are the glossy black-and-whites interspersed with newspaper cutouts and a blown up photo of Pink in a white suit sitting in a regal chair. Jesus Christ and I are the only white guys in the room, figuratively speaking of course.

"That's me and junior, right before the Mike Weaver fight, in Vegas," says the Bossman.

He points a bony finger in the direction of a small black-and-white photo tacked to the wall. The photo shows him looking much the same as he does now, sitting next to his son, who wears a smile, huge biceps, and training togs. Looking very much unlike the heroin addict that he was at the time.

"I was with him for most of the big fights," the Bossman adds.

"Did it make you nervous, watching him fight?"

"It was worse on television," he says. The Bossman is bright and sharp for his age. "When you're watching the fights in person you know exactly what's going on. I was there for Witherspoon, Weaver, Tyson . . ." his voice trails off as he becomes distracted by something on television. "I wasn't surprised when he became a fighter really," says the

Bossman. "He was whupping everything in the neighborhood as a kid."

"Heyyy Ted!" I hear Pinklon's voice and turn around in time for a handshake and a hug. Ever the training freak, he looks like he could still lace them up. In fact, he looks leaner than he did when he struggled at the end of his career against guys like Tommy Morrison and Riddick Bowe.

He sits next to his father on the sofa, and I get a feel for what Thomas will look like in about 40 more years. Mike Tyson's image flickers on the television—the subject of a news story on his myriad legal troubles. Mike Tyson the icon. Mike Tyson the common criminal. Mike Tyson, the man who has to fight to pay off debts. The media loves this stuff.

"Pink, there's Tyson."

I could think of nothing more intelligent to say. I wondered if he would be interested in seeing one of his contemporaries on television, his failures going public whereas my subject's failures were kept largely private. Pinklon gives a dismissive wave without so much as a look at the television. He continues tying his shoelaces.

"Hey Ted, you look like you've been in the gym," he says, giving me the once over.

This, of course, makes me smile.

BROTHER HANDSHAKE MAN.

His real name is Bobby Kaiser. "Bobby runs the gym at Jefferson High School," Pinklon informs me as I wheel my Toyota into the lot. There are fences around everything here—as if to remind you that everything on the premises can and will be stolen. The retro appearance of the school is less a fashion statement, like in suburbia, but more a testament to the nauseating lack of funding in these schools. If I were more of a man, perhaps I would write a book on this. Instead I troll stadiums, chasing athletes around for a quote. I begin to feel the pit-of-my-stomach rumble that I always get when I meet a man who has really done something with his life.

"Bobby was my coach. He taught me how to train."

Brother Handshake Man is "the biggest little man you'll ever meet." He is little, around five feet two inches on a tall day, I suppose. He is one of those ageless men—he could be 35 or 65 for all I know. But he mentions that he has been at the school, coaching and running the gym, since 1968. I do the math and discover that he's no kid. He pumps my hand and smiles, leading us past the group of cornrowed black men outside his office playing chess. I feel like I have a free pass into the inner sanctum. I feel proud to be around him. He shakes my hand again.

"I grew out instead of up!" Kaiser howls while patting his ample belly. He leaves for a moment and returns with an armload of cold juice drinks.

"Bobby, how many kids would you say you put through college all these years?" Pinklon asks.

Kaiser again rubs his belly and removes the black horn rimmed glasses that give him the look of an activist. This guy is a cross between a cartoon character and Malcolm X. Kaiser, I learned, served as a mentor for Pinklon, coaching him in track, football, and basketball through junior high school. And according to the Bossman, Kaiser traveled with Thomas to each of his professional fights until he won the title.

"I think I lost count . . . 50 . . . maybe more. I took the kids on a tour of the South every year. I took them to the black colleges down there. I would pile them in a van and drive all day and all night to get there. Last year I got home from that drive and the gym was spinning! That's when I knew it was time to retire!"

Brother Handshake unleashes a belly laugh and slaps both of our hands. He comes by his nickname honestly.

"Pinklon, you remember that football field?" he says, gesturing out the open door. "That's where we made you a man."

Thomas throws an arm around his old coach while they reminisce.

"Coach Kaiser brought me out of the darkness and into the light."

We all reflect on this for a moment, drinking our juice. I'm about to ask them to elaborate about the darkness, but I realize this isn't a time to talk about hard things, rather, a time to reminisce and tell stories. The men clearly enjoy performing for me.

"Pinklon Thomas was special. The day I met him I knew he was going to be special. He just stood out. Everywhere we went he stood out. He could have been world class in any sport—basketball, track, football, you name it. He was running 9.8 seconds in the hundred-yard dash in eighth grade. He had the natural stamina that all great athletes have. He got caught up in some craziness, but I think we all did back then . . . we all had our share of craziness. But these kids have to have real friends . . . they have to have people in their lives they can talk to."

Craziness, I begin to discover, is code for drugs, women, booze, and violence. It's the word one uses when one doesn't want to talk about it. I file this away for future reference.

"Pinklon never showed me that side of his personality [the drugs]. He always kept it hidden from me," says Kaiser. "I was always impressed with his heart. He was brave to a fault—always on the edge. Each day was like a melodrama to get through, but he was always a loveable guy. Pinklon would never initiate conflict with anyone, but he was always up to a challenge."

I ask Kaiser why he ultimately left the fight game.

"I met too many legendary trainers in that game with drinking and drug problems. I worked 30 years in the factory, and they send me $3,000 a month to sit at home now!"

He stops to slap both of our hands, unleashing a belly laugh. Not a bad deal.

"But I showed Pinky the bright side. That the darkest part of midnight must give way to the brightest part of the morning. I had to walk into some dark places and beg for his life. I had to ask people not to kill him—people I'd known for a long time."

"Let me tell you a story," Pinklon says. "I remember this basketball trip, we had gone to an all-white town to play an all-white school, and we were just getting killed by the referees, man, we weren't getting any calls. And Coach Kaiser, boy, he was getting pissed, we were practically having to hold him back."

By now the two men are up out of their chairs demonstrating.

"Then Coach Kaiser rolled up his sleeves, and that's when I knew it was on."

"Yeah, we had this guy we brought along, a white guy that was sitting at the scorer's table," says Kaiser. "He was our guy but nobody knew it. Anyway, this referee comes over to the table and says to him, 'We really got those niggers, didn't we?'

"And my friend, he says, 'I'm with those niggers.'"

"I CAN REMEMBER A TIME when I was 14 or so, I was using. We would go down to the basement and shoot drugs and throw the needles behind the freezer. My mother found one and wrote me a note and left it by my bed. Made me feel pretty bad."

This is perhaps the understatement of a lifetime. I'm visiting with Pinklon now at Pete's Coney Island—a neighborhood hot dog place with walls papered with black-and-whites of Detroit celebrities, mostly athletes. There is something about the black-and-white, on the cafe wall, that makes the athletes look like gods. It's a little piece of immortality.

"I introduced you to Albert Hatchette before . . . he represented a couple guys . . . a couple guys had contracts on my life. I stuck up their houses. They were out to get me. They . . . thought I had killed some racketeer, which I didn't. I was 12 or 14. We were also in the papers as the 'country club bandits.' We would hide in the bushes at the golf courses and

mug golfers as they came by . . . I made her old, man.
I watched my mother age. I wish I could bring her
back, man . . . she could tell you some stories. She remembers every fight . . . and she's got a story about
every family that lived in every house on that street."

Perhaps my stunned silence prompted him to add:
"It doesn't faze me much to talk about it . . . I've
talked about it a lot."

Thankfully, a young cook—a white kid with long
hair and a ball cap—approaches and asks to shake
the champ's hand. Fame is also a powerful drug, I
think, because it gives people a little hope. Or it least
it seems to make them happy in the moment.

"You really made that little girl's day," the waiter
says, "I could tell she was scared to talk to you, but I
told her just to go on over."

Thomas has just finished signing an autograph
for a shy girl and her mother, who clearly recognizes
him. Pinklon asks the kid if they need another glossy
photo for the restaurant.

Pinklon Thomas turned pro in 1979 after only a
handful of amateur fights, decisioning journeyman
Ken Arlt in Seattle, WA. His mother, blind and in
the advanced stages of diabetes, was on hand for his
pro debut.

"I remember having my mother down for my first
fight. It was August 29, 1978. I have it someplace on
8mm film. I can remember my mom calling, 'Come
on, Junior! Come on, Junior!' She started losing her
sight a couple of months later and never saw another
fight. When you lose your mama, you lose something
very special. She was my greatest supporter and my

greatest strength. I remember walking with her down the street, to the grocery store. I hurt her so much in my life. I have no regrets today—I was young and I didn't really understand my addiction and how I was caught up into it. Right now, today, I really miss Mom. She was there to talk to me when I asked her.

"I think Arlt had had a few fights at the time, but I was able to beat him over six rounds. It was the toughest six rounds I ever fought though. My trainer at the time, Joe West, had told me to not fool around and stay away from my wife before I fought. I gave in two days before the fight. I really felt it and I made the fight a lot harder than it should have been. I won, but I didn't have much fight in me. He was about 230 or 240, out of Portland. I fought him for six rounds—toughest fight of my life. I skipped right over the four-rounders. Being with my wife sapped all of the energy I had stored from training. I beat him with my left jab, and every round I felt like I didn't have another round in me."

The girl with the autograph and her mother are packing it up to leave the little restaurant.

"Hey, you be good, okay," Pinklon calls after the girl.

She doesn't turn or look back.

Thomas got his first big break as a last-minute fill-in for Randall "Tex" Cobb in a televised bout against James "Quick" Tillis in 1982. He upset the rugged Tillis and then went on to fight former two-time title challenger Gerrie Coetzee, the South African who would later win the WBA title, in January of 1983 (also on network TV), to a draw. After a few more wins, it was on to his first world heavy-weight championship bout, vs. Tim Witherspoon in August, 1984. Thomas won the WBC world heavy-weight title from Witherspoon in a 12-round major-ity decision that many ringside observers felt should really have been unanimous. Thomas's only defense, in which he emerged victorious, was a one-punch knockout of Mike Weaver (poleaxing Weaver with a straight right hand) to defend his crown in eight rounds, in June of 1985. After losing to Trevor Berbick in his second defense in March of 1986 (12-round unanimous decision loss in which he looked passive and lethargic), the better part of his career was behind him. In many ways, the fight with Tillis, the wins over Witherspoon and Weaver, and a draw with hard-punching South African Gerrie Coetzee are the best representative samples of Thomas's work. His left jab was considered among the best in boxing, and Thomas used it with regularity in those bouts.

After the Tyson fight, Thomas was used primarily as a big-name trial horse, as his offensive perfor-mances lagged but his chin remained. He sustained brutal defeats at the hands of future champions Evan-der Holyfield and Riddick Bowe, and a one-round stoppage by Tommy Morrison effectively signaled the end of his boxing career.

MIKE TYSON AND Pinklon Thomas are standing on a makeshift podium at the Las Vegas Hilton in 1987. Between them stands Don King in all his bombastic glory. King is rambling on, making bold statements about the fight, in what has turned out to be a boxing tradition of sorts. The pre-fight presser is the place for all things promotional and ridiculous.

Thomas extends his left hand toward Tyson and says, "I'm going to use my jab to snatch that gold right out yo' mouth."

To which Tyson responds, "Fuck you Pink. Suck my dick."

MY FRIENDS ARE naturally curious about this project and often they ask to see old fight films, no doubt to try to place faces with names. Today, a youth minister and a theologian are in my living room and we have decided to watch the May 30, 1987, fight between Mike Tyson and Pinklon Thomas. The youth minister has no interest in boxing, and the theologian, I've just discovered, is quite a fight fan. As it turns out, he wrote a collection of poems in the mid 1990s entitled *The Ballad of Jerry Quarry*. There are closeted boxing fans in every walk of life, it seems. Our wives are in the other room working on lunch.

They all comment on how old Pinklon looks. He does. His body doesn't look nearly as hard and conditioned as it did for Coetzee or even Berbick. He looks thinner. His hair and moustache are both untrimmed. He looks like a fighter on the way out, but is only 29 and will fight for another six years.

Tyson, meanwhile, is in his prime.

Tyson came out fast in the 1st round—presumably reacting to the boos and bad press he got as a result of a clinch-filled bout he had with Bonecrusher Smith. This was the headhunting Tyson, and it appeared as though he would get his 1st-round knockout. Tyson, at the time was described as a two-beat fighter—feint left, feint right, and then he's inside destroying your body with hooks and your chin with uppercuts. Dundee's logic and fight plan was to break Tyson's rhythm. Hit him with a hard jab before he could get into his two-beat cadence. Frustrate him. Get him to stop moving his head and start looking for bombs from the outside.

Thomas succeeded in doing so for much of the early rounds. After weathering a Tyson storm in the 1st round, Thomas relaxed and went about the business of "being first," as Dundee said in the corner between rounds. "Always be first."

Thomas frustrated Tyson by sticking his still-formidable jab in Tyson's face before he could get into his feint-feint-throw rhythm. For the first time in a long time, Tyson looked human, and Thomas was doing it without hugging or running.

Interestingly, this is the only tape that Pinklon Thomas watches himself, and the only tape that he will show guests. Out of all of the impressive wins and knockouts on his resume, he shows the one that reads "TKO by 6" on the ring record.

A visit from the ringside physician between the second and third rounds sends Angelo Dundee over the edge.

"Get the fuck away from this man!" he screams as the doctor tries to get a glimpse at Thomas's eye.

"Am I cut?" Thomas asks.

"No, you're fine, but he's butting the heck out of you" he replies. And for good measure, to the ring doctor: "Get the fuck out of here."

Dundee, something of an amateur psychologist, wanted nothing to come between him and selling his fighter on the fact that he could survive in the same ring with Tyson.

In the ring Pinklon begins to work the jab and my friends are impressed—they expected to see another Tyson execution. Bang. Boom. Thirty seconds and out. And then after the fifth, another distraction. It seems that something has happened to Pinklon's glove, and he's standing in his corner with the glove off.

Pinklon told me that the tab that attaches the thumb to the rest of the glove had split. Angelo Dundee, when I asked him about it, changed the subject.

At any rate—whether Dundee was buying his man some time to rest (Dundee was known to employ such tactics as loosening the ropes for Ali later in his career, to give him an advantage, or manufacturing a distraction in the corner to give his man some rest), or whether gloves actually come undone during the middle of a match—the distraction seemed to hurt Thomas and break his rhythm.

During the break, Tyson could be seen sitting in his corner, trainer Kevin Rooney whispering into his ear. His voice would rise occasionally and one could hear the words "bad intentions" come from his mouth. He had his hand wrapped around Tyson's head as he talked. The whole thing looked very gentle. They looked like brothers or best friends.

Thomas uses the glove story as the reason for his loss, and he's sticking to it. Dundee, ever the master psychologist, in addition to buying his man some time seems to have bought him an excuse as well. Thomas, in his mind, had Tyson right where he wanted him before the glove fell apart.

"He and Kevin Rooney were sucking all the air out of the place," Thomas recalls. "Tyson was over there getting his wind back and I was just getting frustrated."

The bell rang, and a matter of seconds into the 6th round, Pinklon Thomas got caught in a flurry of bad intentions; his head jerking violently as a result of Tyson's hooks and uppercuts. A Tyson shot to his midsection was one of the most wicked body shots in heavyweight boxing history and, according to one Florida boxing personality, "should have stopped Pinklon's heart." Unfortunately, this is the Pinklon Thomas that most people remember. In an interesting turn of events, Tyson is the hard-luck case now—fighting to pay off debtors, bloated, slow, and over-weight. His will no doubt be the classic boxing tragedy.

Later, even after Buster Douglas, Tyson would call it the toughest fight he ever had.

The days following the fight would prove tougher still for Thomas, who went on a week-long bender, looking for heroin in South Central Los Angeles. He tells me the story as we weave through evening traffic in Orlando, the tail lights of the car in front of us casting an eerie glow on his face.

"I was driving down into Compton after the Tyson fight, driving a brand new Cadillac with a .38

and about $10,000 in cash under the armrest. I was looking for dope. I came up on this line of cars, lined up several cars deep, and up the road there were a bunch of young guys in bandanas, a human chain, waving their guns in broad daylight. They were pulling people out of the cars and stealing them, one after another. I pulled up and started talking tough. You have to know how to talk to these people, Ted. I said, 'I just need some fucking dope.' One of the guys recognized me and said, 'Hey man, ain't you that fighter?' I told him I didn't know what the fuck he was talking about, but he waved me through, and I ended up in a crack house where I didn't eat or sleep for days.

"I finally left with an 8-ball and several thousand bucks in the passenger's seat of the car. I wasn't seeing straight but started driving anyway. The last thing I remember was ending up in a ditch, with a Mexican man pulling me out of the car and setting me back in the driver's seat. He asked me if I was okay, and didn't touch the money or the dope. He must have been an angel."

"I think I scared him straight—I think I scared the bejesus out of him one night," says Angelo Dundee by telephone in a later interview. "He came in after being gone for three or four days. He looked miserable. Disheveled. I honestly thought he was just drunk, but I read him the riot act—I told him not to call me, and to forget about it (working together). I think that scared him straight, because I never had another problem."

Dundee, I'm finding, is boxing's eternal optimist. He is either unaware of the extent of the drug problems or simply chooses not to dwell.

"Pinklon always carried himself well. He was a great after-dinner speaker and a great dresser. He always impressed people and still does . . . I think his boxing career was just the beginning for him. Pink's a man of big character.

"We had a great time, Pinklon and I. We got along famously—not an ounce of problems. We worked hand-in-glove. Ask him to tell you about how we used to have good times."

IT IS A RANDOM, hot night in Miami in 1989, and Pinklon Thomas is at a crossroads. Actually, he's sitting in a car outside a smoke house at 1 A.M. He needs drugs but is out of money. The city burns around him as Miami's black community riots over a cop who shot a black kid on a motorcycle.

"I went through about $7,000 that week," he recalls. "The smokehouse was at the corner of 79th St. and 2nd Ave. I had just lost to Holyfield in December of '88 and was out chasing that dope every night."

Holyfield beat Thomas badly in that fight—a fight which truly signaled my subject's decline from fringe title contender to washed-up trial horse. Thomas's reflexes were slowed by years of hard fights and dope, and his ability to get out of the way was gone. Only a tough chin—a great set of whiskers—remained. Not good enough to win hard fights, just good enough to get you seriously hurt. Holyfield, on the other hand, was on a mission. Young and hungry.

Just up from cruiserweight and looking to leave his mark on the head of an old champion. He gave Thomas a horrible beating, until his corner mercifully stopped the fight in the 7th. They should have stopped it much earlier.

On this night, in Miami, Thomas had been awake for seven days and seven nights.

"I was standing there on the street looking at my car, a 1987 Pontiac, wondering if they would give me a half a gram of dope for it."

Thinking the better of selling his car, Thomas got in and began to drive toward home, only to turn back after a few blocks.

"I got in my car again and headed toward home, but I ended up turning back again. I got in my car again, starting driving toward my condo, and then turned back again. Finally I just prayed to God to take me home. When I went into my condo, it was completely torn up. Dishes piled in the kitchen. Empty wine bottles everywhere. I just wanted to come down. I had been awake for seven days. So I found a half bottle of wine and just chugged it down."

Thomas would sleep for 36 hours, only to be awakened by a call from Angelo Dundee's office. He was expected to do fight commentary on a televised card that night.

"I looked horrible. I was 13 pounds underweight, with bags under my eyes. My fingernails were all black from scraping the residue out of crack pipes. None of my clothes fit me. My smallest suit was huge on me—it was a suit I'd had tailored for me overseas. The neck was about an inch too big. I looked like a scarecrow. All I could do was look in the mirror and shake my head.

"So I drove to Angelo's office building and sat in my car for a while. I couldn't stand the thought of walking through that building where everyone knew me and called me champ.

"Betty, Angelo's secretary, saw me first and said, 'Pink, you look terrible.' I told her I couldn't stop using cocaine and she told me I needed help."

Dundee listened from his desk.

"Angelo never looked up from his paperwork, and all he said was, 'Betty, give Pinklon his files and empty his safety deposit box downstairs. And Pink— forget my name and my number.'

"Betty walked me out of the building and gave me a kiss on the cheek. She told me to get some help."

"I went back to my apartment and cried."

WE ARE DRIVING with the whole family now, Thomas and his wife DJ in the front, myself and his two daughters, Patrice and Piara, in the back. They are showing me the hip-hop ring tones on their cell phone, and Pink is weaving his way through rush hour Orlando traffic, the late-model Volvo careening from lane to lane. Thomas is alternately cursing the traffic and engaging in an ongoing good-natured argument with his daughters about their musical tastes. They flip to the hip-hop channel, he flips back to oldies. The girls seemed thrilled that their white passenger knows some lyrics; truthfully, I'm just trying to disctract myself from the thought of dying on the highway with Pinklon Thomas. I don't want to go out like this. Piara immerses herself in an acting class project while Patrice attempts to convince her dad that she needs her own apartment next year at junior college. It is like a scene from the Cosby show, save for the fact that their dad is a recovering dope addict and a former heavyweight champ.

Pinklon Thomas has been clean for over 15 years, and we have spent the day talking largely about his sobriety. We visited the juvenile detention center (The Center for Drug Free Living) where he works as a counselor, and saw the orange-jumpsuited black kids in the sliders (prison slang for the sandals the inmates are issued). The kids flock to him, not only because he is famous, but because he clearly enjoys them. He is the perfect combination of hard-ass and compassion.

"Today I can honestly say I am a very happy man," he says. "Happily married. I enjoy my work. In my era a lot of guys came up and went out the wrong way—whether it was lifestyle or having problems financially or what have you. I started with the center in '93 and am still here in 2004 doing pretty much the same kind of work. I have kids' parents call me all the time to ask me about addiction. Recovery to me is the ultimate accomplishment in my life. And my belief in God was the greatest thing that came over me."

Pinklon Thomas is clearly the guy for this job, but it's a job he seems to want desperately to lose. Pinklon Thomas wants to be famous again. Book tours. Speaking engagements. Maybe a film. Just get the story out there, it will sell itself. Unfortunately, when Pinklon Thomas becomes famous again, he will probably give up the only job he ever had that means something.

Soon we roll up to Medieval Times, a suburban Florida institution of faux ponds, a faux castle, and faux fight scenes between knights and warriors. James, a guy I met earlier at Pink's gym, has given us the hookup on tickets. We are late, so there is some confusion as to whether the tickets are still here. James was the token white guy at Pinklon's gym—a fact which we bonded over between rounds on the heavybag. I would guess that every white fighter, at one time or another, has been the token white guy at his gym. James is emceeing the event and has traded his gym clothes for a regal purple robe and a crown. After donning our paper hats and crossing the moat, we are seated.

There is a meal of roast chicken, rolls, a pork tenderloin, and coffee available for an extra six dollars. Pinklon remarks that it had better be the best coffee in the world before ordering a cup, as caffeine is his only drug these days. A table wench appears and snaps our picture, which will be made available later for the tidy sum of twenty-five dollars. After the battle James takes the mike again and begins honoring the groups and individuals in the castle—the noble insurance agents from State Farm, Sir Timmy's sixth birthday party, etc. There is polite clapping. Finally, he introduces one of the "bravest champions in boxing history, Pinklon Thomas." More clapping.

The lobby clears quickly after the show, and Pinklon sticks around to sign autographs. James and the other knights have made their way home to the apartment complexes and condos where knights live when not waging war at Medieval Times. A little girl makes her way toward Pinklon, nervously, and asks who he is. When he says "Pinklon Thomas," she looks satisfied and turns on her little kid heels to walk away, although I'm certain she has no idea who he is. I am waved into a large group—with Pink, DJ, and his daughters—for one last picture. The camera snaps and for a moment we are the perfect American family.

CHAPTER EIGHT

TYRELL **BIGGS**

*There is required for the composition of a great
commander not only massive common sense and
reasoning power, not only imagination, but also
an element of legerdemain, an original and
sinister touch, which leaves the enemy puzzled as
well as beaten.*

—WINSTON CHURCHILL, *THE WORLD CRISIS*

ON THE NIGHT BEFORE his fight with Tyrell Biggs,
Mike Tyson is oddly silent. He didn't say a word at
the weigh-in and was silent at the press conference as
well, where his manager Jim Jacobs had words with
Biggs manager Lou Duva. Jacobs felt that Duva had
broken a handshake agreement between the two
camps, in which Duva agreed to not address any
comments directly at Tyson in the pre-fight festivities.
Duva commented that his guy would teach Tyson a
thing or two about boxing. Jacobs, all bets now off,
replied by questioning the mental capacity and readi-
ness of Biggs. Chaos ensued.

"I found the press conference entertaining and distasteful," said Tyson, the final speaker.

Tyson's distaste for Tyrell Biggs dates back to the amateurs, where he felt that Biggs received superstar treatment, while he was treated as a second-class citizen. Because of amateur boxing's aversion to Cus D'Amato and his penchant for training fighters to be knockout artists instead of preparing them for the peck-and-run amateurs, Tyson was forced to fight in the heavyweight (under 200) division, while Biggs got glory and Olympic gold at super heavyweight. Tyson, however, was left only with a loss (to Henry Tillman, now incarcerated, whom he would later knock out as a pro) and a great deal of resentment.

Finally, from the back of the limousine carrying Tyson and his corner back to their quarters, Tyson is asked how he feels going into the bout.

His reply: "If I don't kill him, it don't count."

FIFTY-SEVENTH AND Haverford in Philly, 9:15 P.M. This is where I am supposed to meet Tyrell Biggs for the first time. I have just driven ten hours in pouring rain that lasted from my front porch in Lansing, MI, to here. If I was less tired, I would probably be more scared, but as it is I just eat junk food and decide not to think about what an easy mark I am right now. As one drives farther from the center of Philadelphia, out to these neighborhoods, the buildings get shabbier and the streets get darker as the city decides that certain amenities, like lights, are non-essentials in the ghetto. Downtown's trechcoats and trendy bars turn into dirty jackets and liquor stores—alcohol no longer being a vehicle for networking and socializing, and more just a tool for dulling the pain and getting by until tomorrow. Mine is the only white face for blocks. I pull up in front of an apartment building, my car idling, and dial Biggs. "Stay in your car," he says, "I'll walk to the end of the street." I wait there for him for what seems like an eternity while people walk by. I turn the radio on and off about 100 times. I self-chastise for feeling afraid. But there's a church across the street, and I could probably get help there if I needed to. Where the hell is Biggs? My phone buzzes again, and I look over my left shoulder to see Biggs approaching the car. He looks just like he did in the films, his face surprisingly uncrushed (besides the ordinary lumps of scar tissue over each eye) by a life-time in boxing. He has the same high-top fade that he had in the films, and I always though that, like Ali, his soft features were more befitting a film star than a fighter. We shake hands. "It's great to finally meet you," he says.

Incidentally, Biggs is the only fighter I have inter-viewed for this project who asked me about my back-ground—where I'm from, how I got involved with boxing, etc. His voice is a deep baritone, and, clearly, conversation is something that he enjoys. I am ner-vous talking—filling him in on the drive, etc. He often responds to my statements with the word "cool." Biggs has the huge, scarred hands of a fighter and is wearing sweats and a black T-shirt underneath a winter coat.

After chatting in the street for a few minutes, we are now cruising through the streets where Tyrell

Biggs grew up and now lives again. He is folded, accordion-like, into my tiny Toyota Echo. We are looking for a place to talk, as the gym where he works with kids as a recreation specialist has closed for the night. The storefronts that aren't boarded up have pulled down their metal grates for the evening, and we finally settle on Mimi's, a pizzeria just a block or two from where Biggs lives with his father.

"My dad used to take me up to Deer Lick, which is about an hour or so outside of Philly, to watch Muhammad Ali train," Biggs says. "He took me up there when I was a kid, before the George Foreman fight, and I was expecting to see Ali gliding around the ring, sticking and moving, you know, doing the Ali thing. And do you know what he did? For about ten rounds he laid up on the ropes and let his sparring partners pound away at him. I remember being disappointed, but that was the beginning of the rope-a-dope style that he used to beat Foreman. It was funny, man.

"My dad was a male nurse," says Biggs. "But he loved the fights. He fought in the army, and he used to always take me along when he would go to the Monday Night Fights at the Spectrum. I was the youngest, so I suppose I had to go whether I wanted to or not, it was like, 'Hey, you're going with me.' But after the second time or so, I started liking it. When I was about ten, he said, 'Hey, you wanna box?' I said, 'Sure, I'll give it a try.' He bought me a heavy bag and a speed bag for the basement, and I would go home and try out the moves that I saw at the fights."

Biggs would dabble in the sport as a middle schooler, but it was basketball that originally brought acclaim and a college scholarship at Hampton to the six-foot four-inch Biggs.

"I didn't like college life at all," he says. "I lasted about a semester, but I was big into the drug thing, or whatever, at the time. To me it was just a big party. That pretty much demolished the basketball. By that time a fella named Steve Hall was helping me out . . . he bought me my equipment—a rope, my wraps and gloves. It just took off from there basically."

Biggs would return to Philadelphia looking for something to do. He remembered boxing and eventually made his way to Joe Frazier's gym, where he made their amateur team and began winning the fights that capture the attention of the US Olympic Committee.

"I made the Joe Frazier amateur boxing team, and we fought the Muhammad Ali team. Marvis [Frazier] was the top heavyweight, of course, and he fought Tony Tubbs . . . and I fought the coheavyweight fight against a guy named Curtis. Marvis got beat, but I won my heavyweight fight. That caught the attention of the Olympic team, and a few months later, I got an invitation to go out to Colorado Springs and train for a tournament in Ireland."

I ask Biggs about his Olympic training center experience and its difference from the Philadelphia streets.

"It was easy for me to adjust to that environment," he says. "You were living right there on the grounds with all of the other athletes, so it was a positive environment. I pretty much stayed out there and competed with the USA team. I won three or four ABF championships and won most of my international fights. Of course, the training was great at altitude. Training at altitude, in Colorado Springs, was a big advantage, conditioning-wise, once it came time to fight. In the 3rd round I would still be fresh, whereas most of my opponents were slowing down."

I ask Biggs what his drug use looked like in the Olympic years.

"I would generally use between fights and get clean, leave it alone long enough to win my fights," says Biggs of his drug use. "But then, naturally, after a win I would want to celebrate, so I'd go back and use it. Peer pressure is how I got caught up in that . . . surrounding myself with the wrong people."

Biggs, not Tyson, was the Olympic committee's choice to represent the United States as a super heavyweight at the 1984 Olympic Games in Los Angeles, a decision they made long before the games and did a very poor job of keeping secret. Biggs would join a legendary Olympic team that included Evander Holyfield, Virgil Hill, Meldrick Taylor, and Pernell Whitaker. He traveled to Ireland and Cuba for amateur tournaments. At a match with the Cubans, the United States was 1–12, with Biggs notching the only win of the tournament, "against the guy who beat Teofilo Stevenson." He recalls that the Cuba trip was the first time he remembers feeling the pangs of resentment from his teammates.

"There was a lot of stuff going on back then that I wasn't aware of at the time," he says. "The guys were kind of envious of that win in Cuba."

"He [Tyson] had a problem with me because the Olympic people were set on me being the super heavyweight. He had to cut weight and ended up losing against Henry Tillman. I don't blame him for being upset."

The committee had the foresight to test Biggs for drugs in Colorado well before the games, as they had a hint of his lifestyle, instead of in Los Angeles, as was customary. The test, a positive, led to the counseling that would eventually put Biggs on the road to recovery and save him from the "catastrophe" of being disqualified from Olympic competition.

"It really helped seeing a doctor guy, and working through the different aspects of what I went through," he recalls.

The fighter just celebrated his 20th year of sobriety and celebrated by calling the doctor who helped him get clean.

"At different times I would call him, over the holidays or whatever, and he would tweak my brain and ask me questions to make sure I was on the right track. If you don't want to do it, you won't do it. You only do stuff you want to do. I've always been able to be open with him, and he would give me the tools to self-counsel. Now I try to get the kids to stop smoking weed around the Center and then add into it why they don't need to be doing it anywhere. And that helps me because I'm hearing the things that I need to hear when I say it to the kids. I was in California once, and I heard a guy give a 'don't do drugs' talk to a bunch of kids and the next day he got busted. That's not going to happen to me."

Unfortunately, Biggs and the rest of the US boxing team would not be able to test themselves against the best of the best, as the Soviet boycott of the games left Cuba, and Teofilo Stevenson, at home.

"I knew I would've beaten Stevenson anyway," said Biggs in a *KO Magazine* interview. "But he's not here, so all I can do is win."

Biggs, born December 22, 1960, in Philadelphia, won the gold medal at the 1984 Olympics in Los Angeles, CA, fighting in the super-heavyweight division. Biggs outslicked rugged Italian Francesco Damiani, scoring a 4–1 decision to win gold. Like all Olympic champions, he was made by the networks to look perfect in soft focus. Their athlete-friendly features masked a growing dependence on drugs and a cocaine addiction that would inhibit the fighter's ability to stake claim to a title in the professional ranks. But Biggs was tall, good looking, had a great jab; and would turn pro at a time when professional boxing was still mourning the loss of the charismatic and talented Muhammad Ali. His replacements weren't exactly capturing the fight fan's imagination.

Biggs signed with Lou Duva and Shelly Finkel and turned professional soon after his Olympic victory, scoring a 6-round, unanimous decision over Mike Evans on November 15, 1984, at Madison Square Garden in New York City in his first bout. He was booed that night, by a crowd who had entered for free. They expected to see heavyweight fireworks, but instead saw a Biggs who was overly cautious and content to jab and move against inferior competition. Six weeks after the bout, he would check himself into the Care Unit Hospital in Orange, California, for treatment of alcohol and drug abuse. It was rumored that he was bothered by the fans' negative reaction to his debut.

"Ty couldn't handle the negativism," said Finkel in a *New York Times* interview. "He put in all that time and effort in training, but he still got booed. I don't think his fragile ego could handle it."

I ask Biggs if he felt like he was ever truly understood, during the more famous periods of his life. He was roundly criticized in boxing publications such as *Ring Magazine* and *KO Magazine* for his apparent lack of focus and an unwillingness to come forward and brawl.

"It was totally surreal. People just knew the boxing, of course not. You're made out to have this persona . . . and, you know, of course not. By no means was I the typical Philadelphia fighter . . . style-wise and even how I started in the sport, learning to fight in the amateurs. Most of these were straight street-guys who went right to the pros."

Biggs was criticized for the jab and run tactics he had honed in the amateurs, where scoring points—not knockouts—was the way to victory. "KOs aren't important," national amateur coach Pat Nappi had told Biggs. "Just win."

He went on to face fighters such as Lennox Lewis, Riddick Bowe, and Buster Mathis Jr., losing to each before ending his career with a 2nd-round knockout of Carlton Davis on August 27, 1998, in Atlanta, GA. His professional ring record was 30 wins (20 knockouts) and 10 losses in 40 contests.

"It was almost surreal, winning the gold medal," says Biggs. "Surreal" is a word he uses often to describe his life. There is a buzz in the air at Mimi's; several of the patrons have gathered around our table to eavesdrop.

"Standing up on that podium, there is no high, no drink, no drugs, and no kind of substance that compares to what I felt that night, when they raised the American flag and played "The Star Spangled Banner." It's indescribable. I remember in 1976 Ray Leonard said that it was unexplainable, and after I won I knew what he was talking about. I heard him when I said that.

"They had a welcome-home, congratulations kind of a thing for me here in Philly, where they closed down a couple of blocks. A lot of people were blown away because last they knew I was off playing basketball. And I remember before the Olympics shooting a 7-11 commercial with four other Olympic hopefuls . . . one of them was Al Oerter, the shot putter. It was one of those '7-11 is giving me the freedom to train and helping me pursue my dreams' type of spots," he remembers, laughing. "But the crazy thing is that I ended up being the only one of the five of us who brought home the gold medal. Ain't that something? That was the theme of the commercial, winning the gold. That's kind of cool."

Biggs sits silently for a moment, remembering. I take the opportunity to look around the parlor at the faces around me—the girl behind the counter, the tough-looking kids on the video game machines, and the guy cleaning up in the corner—everybody is checking us out. I ask Biggs where the gold medal is, and if he looks at it often.

"It's in Texas," he says, matter-of-factly. "It's in a safety deposit box at a bank down there. I was down there doing a photo thing and I put it in there for safekeeping . . . I was planning on keeping it in my room and a guy said that I should put it in a safety deposit box. I just never took it out."

The pizza parlor is closing down around us, and Biggs is greeted by a friend who says he went to grade school with the fighter. Hugs are exchanged and questions are asked. The man asks me for two bucks, to buy a bus ticket, which I produce after some digging. Biggs apologizes profusely after the man leaves, but I do my best to assure him that it is no problem at all. They are pulling the metal grates down in front of Mimi's, and soon we will be back on the street.

"MIKE WAS COMPLETELY relaxed against Biggs. He hit him with punches, elbows, shoulders . . . you name it," says former manager Steve Lott. "If you look at that fight, Biggs' face was really messed up bad."

Biggs and trainer George Benton had concocted a pre-fight plan to use Biggs's formidable jab to break Tyson's rhythm, and then use superior footwork to stay out of range of Tyson's bombs. The idea was to stick and move—leaving Tyson in the center of the ring to be pecked by the jab, setting him up for straight rights and left hooks that would come later. Unfortunately, those punches would never come. The Biggs jab materialized—37 times in round 1—but faded after he took his first significant shots.

"Everybody has a fight plan," said Tyson, "until they're hit."

Tyson, who entered the ring draped in his three championship belts, brought an unblemished record of 31–0, 27 by KO, into Convention Hall in Atlantic City. Biggs, however, stood six feet four inches and weighed 228, and there were some, though few, who felt that he had what it took to beat Tyson.

"Biggs had some different experiences in the amateurs," said Philadelphia boxing historian John DiSanto, a member of the International Boxing Research Organization. "He was always considered a good fighter, but one who had the misfortune of coming up in the era of Mike Tyson. I don't think anybody really thought he had a shot at winning the fight, but in those days nobody did."

Since Muhammad Ali, the public was hungry for another heavyweight rivalry, one that blended styles and had the bad blood necessary to sustain interest. This, some thought, could be that rivalry.

Tyson quickly dispelled that notion. He used impeccable head movement in round 1 to all but neutralize the Biggs jab, leaving him in range to whip the left hooks and body shots that would take apart the taller opponent. Biggs carried his hands curiously low from the opening bell. His left hand was, at all times, down around his waistline, a dangerous move against a quick-handed heavyweight such as Tyson. And as if to dispel any notion that he was there for sport, Tyson whipped an elbow into Biggs's left eye at the end of round 1.

"I thought I had more stuff than him," says Biggs. "I knew he was a great puncher, but I was confident that I could win the fight. But Lou Duva put me on a weight program before the fight because they had done that with Holyfield and it had been successful. I agreed to it because of the power that Tyson had. But Holyfield fought at light heavyweight in the amateurs and had to bulk up, whereas I had my best fight against Jeff Sims at about 217 or 218. I was about 240 or 250 when I fought Tyson and that was weight that I put on over the span of about six or seven months. It was a mistake for that fight because that wasn't my strength, I kind of went against my natural ability. I wish I had trained like I'd trained for the Sims fight."

Biggs, who broke his collarbone in round 1 of the Sims fight, rallied to win a 10-round decision. Biggs bounced and danced on the balls of his feet, effectively beating the muscular Sims with just one arm, giving hope to all who thought they were witnessing the second coming of Muhammad Ali. It was the proudest moment of Biggs's pro career.

"I was hurt, and I knew it was bad, and it was kind of like I could cave into it or I could go out and keep fighting to win the fight," says Biggs of the Sims fight. "But with some, uh, encouragement, from George Benton and Lou Duva in the corner, I knew I could either quit or go after it and win the fight. It was the epitome of boxing for me."

As the Tyson fight wore on, Biggs reverted to a tendency that had shown itself in other fights, that of brawling when hurt. Against David Bey, when he suffered a 32-stitch gash over his left eye, the tactic worked and he scored a 6th-round stoppage. Such tactics would not work against Tyson.

"Because I was so big from the weight training [Biggs fought at 228], it slowed me up and tightened me up. I had trouble getting my punches off."

"I could have knocked him out in the 3rd round," Tyson told writers after the fight. "But I did it very slowly. I wanted him to remember it for a long time. He didn't show any class as a professional boxer, so I made him pay for his actions with his health."

Tyson continued to batter Biggs. His trainer, Kevin Rooney, implored him to do more between rounds, telling him that he was "not doing enough," and not to "mess around with this guy."

By the end Biggs's face was swollen, and blood streamed down the left side of his face, staining his white trunks pink. A left hook blasted Biggs through the ropes toward the end of the 7th and, after getting up briefly, he succumbed to another left hook that sent him to the seat of his trunks before Tony Orlando mercifully stopped the bout. Post-fight, Tyson displayed none of his usual sportsmanship and concern for the opponent—rather, he left Biggs alone in his corner and spoke only to tell reporters and fans that he could have ended it early, preferring rather enjoyably to beat on his opponent.

Tyson's post-fight comments proved to be a rare departure from the carefully crafted suggestions usually given the fighter by Lott, just before the post-fight interview. The comments were a rare look behind the curtain at the rage that at times seemed to fuel Tyson.

"When I would hit him, he was making woman-noises in there," said an excited Tyson. "He was like uggg . . . uggg . . . "

Tyson is smiling, mimicking the sounds of a woman being injured in the throes of passion, or simply being hurt.

"I THINK TYSON'S BASICALLY a good guy," says Biggs. "Generally misunderstood. I remember running into him once out in LA after we fought . . . I was dating a girl and Tyson was dating her sister. I pulled up to the house in my Rolls and Tyson pulled up in his Bentley. He shook my hand and said, 'Hey man, what's happening,' that sort of thing. That was basically the extent of it."

We are driving again, and I'm filling Biggs in on the guys that I have interviewed thus far, as well as my impressions of Tyson as intelligent and gentle, upon meeting him after his fight with Kevin McBride. I theorize that he has made some of the decisions he's made simply because he was taken advantage of so many times along the way.

"Who hasn't been taken advantage of in this sport, though?" Biggs replies. "You get all the hype in boxing about doing your thing and being champion, but nobody says anything about being the ex-champion. It's two different deals, man."

The ex-champion is the most interesting story in boxing, as boxing is generally the only sport that tells the stories of its ex-champions. I ask Biggs whether he was happier then, or now, being back home. I half-expect him to put the usual positive spin on his answer—to talk about how he's learned so much and how he's happier now than ever.

"I was happier back then. I would go back there in a heartbeat," he says, without hesitation, of his Olympic days and early in his pro career. I am a little taken aback by his honesty.

"I was happier then by a long shot. I didn't have the same challenges or worries back then. I didn't have to worry about the bills coming or how much it was, because somebody would always just take care of it. Back then, when I would go into a clothing store or whatever, I didn't ask how much anything cost . . . the question was how many do I want? That's a big lifestyle difference. If I could do it over again, I would have never ever gotten involved in drugs."

We are winding through the neighborhoods now, and settle on the only open place we see, a 24-hour Chinese restaurant.

"Let me give you an example," he says. "Back then I would get on an airplane with a ticket for coach, and they would always move me up to first class because I was a champion. Now, when I get a ticket for coach, I fly coach. I don't get asked to go up to first class anymore!" He laughs. "It took me pretty much by surprise, because most of the good things that happened to me weren't expected anyway. I could have never predicted what happened to me, with the boxing stuff. So many different things and people were coming at me . . . "

Nobody prepares you for that.

"Sometimes I miss boxing," he says, "but not enough to go back and want to do it. I'm too old. Just thinking about the things that I've already done, you know, that's not going to happen anymore. It's already done."

Unfortunately, boxing is unlike most professional sports in that, as athletes, we all come to a point, be it in high school or college, where someone tells is we aren't good enough anymore and that, instead of being participants, we will have to make our peace with enjoying the sport as a fan. Not so with boxing. You can't just go down to the Y and mess around with it. It's all or nothing.

"Some of the guys I fought with are in pretty rough shape; you know—slurring their words and stuff," Biggs continues. "You can hear it on me a little bit . . . but hopefully not too bad. People remember me around here, they know who I am, but sometimes they can be mean and rough. The kids at the Center call me Tyson all the time, because all they know about me is that I fought Tyson. That's mainly what I'm known for—'Yo he's the dude that fought Tyson.'

"But I don't think about how I want to be remembered. You're going to be remembered however you want to be remembered. I know first and foremost that I'm a good person regardless of whatever . . . and that I've always meant well. I never set out to be scandalous."

I ask Biggs about faith.

"It doesn't play as big a role as it probably should, but I pray every night," he says.

What do you pray for?

"I pray for the strength to make it through another day, pretty much, the strength to overlook the negative and just stay positive. To get up and do it all over again."

In fact, Biggs has been up since 6 A.M., and it is nearly 10:30 at night. His morning, and with it another day of work, will come fast, so we begin to wrap up. We talk about life, and about the fact that unlike most of his contemporaries who are born, live, work, and die within the radius of a few Philadelphia blocks, Tyrell Biggs did something extraordinary. And that the most educated and successful men among us, when they turn on the television to watch the Olympics, secretly, someplace deep down, want to be an Olympic gold medalist. To know that on a given day they walked into an arena and were the only one to walk out without losing. That, regardless of current circumstances, is significant. Biggs, a creative person by nature, is speaking now of his other passion, drawing.

"If I could do it all over again, I would have wanted the world to see my art. I can draw, man. Nothing special, just boxing guys and stuff, but I won a little art competition as a kid, it was a football game that I drew, and I always kind of wondered if I could have done something with it. I picked it up from my brother. I admire fashion designers and how they sketch out the clothing . . . trying to design a suit with the perfect lines for their models. I would have liked to create a suit, or tailor a shirt in a certain way. Here, let me give you a quick example. You remember the Flintstones—like Fred and Barney and Wilma?"

He motions for my notepad and pen and begins scribbling. I am in the Philadelphia ghetto, in a Chinese place, with Chinese soap operas playing on the TV, being drawn a picture by the Olympic champion I watched on television as an eight-year-old. Surreal. Biggs scribbles away and hands the pad back over, revealing a detailed Fred Flintstone, complete with boxing glove and extended fist.

"It's a little boxing Fred," he says, smiling. "If I'd had more time, I would have drawn Barney."

We end up in front of Biggs's home, just around the corner from the pizza place, where he lives with his father, who I spoke to several times in setting up the interview. His father, once a fight fan, is now a skeptic and felt more comfortable with the interview taking place elsewhere.

"You know how when you talk on the phone to someone, you get a mental picture of what they look like?" Biggs asks.

Yeah.

"Don't take this the wrong way, but when we talked on the phone to set this thing up, I figured you'd be more of a . . . "

He pauses for a moment, looking for the right word. My mind is already on the challenge of navigating the streets back to my hotel.

"A yuppie."

I thank Biggs, and then let him back out into the Philadelphia night.

THE LARRY HOLMES **INTERLUDE**

I CALL JAY NEWMAN more often than I call my own mother. Newman handles public relations for Larry Holmes Enterprises and seems to serve as something of a gatekeeper for Holmes himself. I dial Newman on a Tuesday morning . . . a Thursday afternoon . . . a Friday just before the close of business hours. Our conversations often go as follows:

Me: "Jay, just following up again on the *Facing Tyson* project. Can't imagine doing this thing without Larry . . . I can come to Easton whenever it's convenient for you." (And probably whenever it's least convenient for me.)

Jay: "Ted, what's your number again [pause while Jay pretends to rifle through his office looking for the number, which I gave him two days ago]? Okay . . . Larry wants to do it, it's just a matter of getting everybody's schedules on the same page. Can you call back next Monday?"

I would be glad to call next Monday, Jay. How are your kids? I talk to you more often than I talk to my wife (ha ha). I call Monday, and Larry, without fail, is in California taping a television show about celebrities learning to ballroom dance. And then he is in Tahoe promoting his new line of Larry Holmes slot machines (seriously, I'm not making that up). And then he is in New York talking to someone about something. Oh, the New York where I was last week, where we could have met for a drink, a coffee, a canoli, a milk. We could have met for anything, but what I have learned from Jay Newman in public relations is that Larry Holmes is always somewhere else. All I want to do is meet him.

The cash, if not the legacy, was there for Larry Holmes. Holmes, the Easton Assassin, was far less assassin and far more the pragmatic businessman. Consequently, he's one of the few 80s heavyweights to have held onto and grown his money over the years. Holmes was boxing's version of the mutual fund—never sexy or glamorous, but always a safe investment.

A visit to the Holmes Web site reveals that everything there is for sale. For a small fee you can own a Larry Holmes signed photograph, an autographed boxing glove—or, for a slightly larger fee, you can even have the real Larry Holmes call your friends on their birthdays and leave a personalized greeting. Also something of a real estate tycoon, Holmes peddles office space through his Web site, where visitors can take a virtual tour of buildings on Larry Holmes Drive. While he possessed neither the personality of Ali nor the violent knockout flash of Tyson, Holmes was nothing if not a shrewd, brutally efficient businessman. He used a stiff jab and sneaky defense to keep opponents at bay, and, later in his career, shrewd matchmaking to keep his faculties intact and keep him in the ring. Holmes will never be considered a "warrior," but he'll also never be punchy and broke.

Holmes, born in Cuthbert, Georgia, began his career as a sparring partner for Muhammad Ali, and, despite one of the best left jabs in boxing and 20 successful title defenses, is probably best known and resented for giving Ali a bad beating at the end of his career. You have the unfortunate good luck to beat up a legend and it takes a long time for the country to forgive. This, along with a heavy handed public relations touch (see "kiss my big black behind" post-Spinks, and "Rocky Marciano couldn't carry my jockstrap"), made it hard for the public to love Larry Holmes. Meanwhile, his refusal to return my calls is making it tough for me to love Larry Holmes.

Holmes retired post-Tyson in 1988, but like all good fighters has unretired several times since. He lost a title fight to Evander Holyfield by decision in 1990 and lost his last title shot to Oliver McCall in 1994 at the tender age of 45. Fortunately for Holmes, to a certain extent he fought like an old fighter even when he was a young fighter, so his style aged well over the years. He even dusted off said style for a payday against Eric (Butterbean) Esch in 2002. Holmes's career record is 69–6 (44 KOs).

CHAPTER NINE

TONY **TUBBS**

*All world-class fighters have ego. Ego is
obligatory. Without it a fighter will not have the
authenticity to do what he must: Dominate
another man by as naked a show of force as his
society permits.*

—PHIL BERGER, *BLOOD SEASON*

I AM IN THE DRESSING ROOM of a 47-year-old man
preparing to fight a professional fight. There are
problems. Nobody can find the mouthpiece, and the
gloves that Tony Tubbs wants to wear, a pair of large
blue Everlasts, are currently being worn in the ring by
co-feature fighter Ravea Springs. They're the only
ones that feel good, he says, the other gloves are all
too tight.

Tubbs is preparing to fight a guy named Jason
Waller from somewhere in Virginia. Waller's record is
28–28–4, and he is a last-minute replacement for
Tubbs's original opponent, who simply decided yesterday not to show up for the fight. This was to be a grand

ring return for Tony's brother Nate Tubbs as well; however, his opponent, unfortunately, is "incarcerated."

The dressing room door is marked "Co-stars" and is a small room with the requisite large mirror with the ball lights and a pleather couch. Through the door stream various members of the Indiana Boxing Commision; most of them wield throwaway cameras and want to snap a pic of the former heavyweight champion. One gets the impression that Indiana boxing commissioners don't spend a whole lot of time around actual boxing, so tonight's event takes on added meaning as a chance to rub shoulders with a real, live professional athletes. Indeed, the whole evening has a retro-night feel. Tony's trunks, his cornerman's satins, and his opponent all look straight out of the 80s.

"I've got a big picture of Tony up in my office," offers a commisioner to nobody in particular. A handler explains that he will be bringing his wife by to see the former champ as well. The man, Nick, goes to find her.

"Nick, I don't want no damn wives in here!" shouts Tubbs down the hall, to no avail. The wives appear a couple of moments later—hair curled and faces heavily made up for a night out at the casino. They stand in the doorway and gawk as Tubbs, still gloveless, shadowboxes in front of the dressing room mirror where countless B-list stars, such as Wayne Newton and Tom Jones, have preened before him. Their pictures line the wall as proof of their presence in the room. As Tubbs throws punches at the mirror, his trainer exclaims, "He's gettin' ready to throw some shit, baby!"

The room, myself included, nods its approval because that just seems appropriate. One would think a 47-year-old man needs all the encouragement he can find. Tubbs looks thin through the shoulders and arms and thick through the waist, like he always did, although to his credit he looks to be more fit than he was when he fought Mike Tyson in 1988. The Jheri-curl of the mid-80s has been replaced by a short Afro, flecked with gray at the temples.

"We gotta get those damn gloves," says Tubbs to the room at large.

Soon I will follow the 47-year-old man out of the dressing room and up to the ring. His mother will pace the perimeter of the ring, nervous, like she has for 25 years.

TONY AND I ARE scheduled to meet at 4:00 at the Picadilly Deli, and he is, unlike most pro athletes, prompt. The Deli is a part of the Grand Victoria Casino lobby, a riverboat affair on the border between Indiana and Ohio, the likes of which have sprung up throughout the Midwest and flourised—giant faux wood and neon structures jutting into the night sky. Its patrons are mostly of the elderly variety and walk right past Tubbs as we occupy a back table. They are on to the greater business of slot machines, roulette wheels, and affordably priced buffet items.

We are introduced by fight promoter Greg Kasse, who looks to be right out of central casting—shirt unbuttoned down to navel, gray chest hair, medallions, and cell phone attachment hanging out of his ear. If the room is even half full tonight, we'll be doing this every other month, Kasse promises. He leaves us to attend to pre-fight matters—one of his undercard fighters is in prison and another needs an HIV test and is trying to find an open clinic. The show starts in three hours. The work of a fight promoter is never done.

Tubbs is accompanied by his manager Clint Calkins, a white guy in his late twenties. Calkins, I learned, used to write fan letters to Tubbs as a teenager and of late encouraged Tubbs to make a comeback as Calkins's first entree into the fight business as a manager. I look for signs of guilt in Calkins, but am slow to pass judgment because, as with most fight people, he is open and accomodating. The fact that he has a 47-year-old man believing he can regain the heavyweight title is a testimony to the power of delusion in sports.

"Clint makes the decisions," says Tubbs. "I told him to go ahead and set me something up so that I can string a few wins together here and maybe break back into the top ten."

"It's important not to overmatch or undermatch, at this point," Calkins adds. He is himself a struggling pro—a cruiserweight, apparently overmatched himself, with a career record of 3–13.

Tubbs is talking with his hands, which I've noticed is something that most fighters do. He uses his large mitts to underscore points and moves them subconsciously throughout the interview as though he were slipping punches. Boxing, clearly, is still a thrill to Tony Tubbs. Just a few hours before the fight, he is jacked.

"The heavyweights out there don't have no boxing skills. I've sparred with the Klitschko brothers and I figured them out. The heavyweights now are all big guys who can punch, but they have no real talent."

I ask Tubbs what draws a 47-year-old man to the ring, besides money.

"It's like I'm fighting you with my mind now," he says. "I'm trying to use feints to set my man up . . . it's like chess. I feint to checkmate."

He is proud of the comment. Calkins chuckles and nods his approval like a fan-turned-manager should. The plan is to move Tubbs out to Iowa after the fight—away from the Cincinnati streets where he battled drug addiction and into the promised land of the Midwestern circuit, where the living is clean and easy wins will be plentiful.

TONY "TNT" TUBBS was born February 15, 1958, and grew up as one of nine children in the projects of Cincinnati. After an impressive amateur career spanning almost 250 fights, he was a favorite to medal in the 1980 Olympics. But the United States boycotted the Games, and Tubbs skipped the trials to turn pro.

Known for his hand speed in a highly competitive heavyweight division during the 1980s, Tubbs debuted as a professional in 1980 and soon defeated fellow prospect Clarence Hill, despite being knocked down in the first round. He beat former Ali nemesis Jimmy Young in 1983, and a victory over future WBA champ James "Bonecrusher" Smith earned Tubbs a shot at the WBA title. He won a unanimous decision over Greg Page on April 29, 1985, in Buffalo to capture the WBA championship. Nine months later, he lost it in a split decision to Tim Witherspoon on January 17, 1986.

In many ways, Tubbs could be a poster child for the heavyweight division's "lost period" between Muhammad Ali and Mike Tyson. Like many of his contemporaries, Tubbs had drug problems and trouble committing to a sport for which he showed tremendous aptitude.

Tubbs's lack of focus caused him to enter fights out of shape, dulling his once sharp reflexes and hurting his ability to go long rounds.

Mike Tyson knocked him out in two rounds in 1988, in a fight that took place in Tokyo, Japan.

"I didn't have too much time to get ready for the fight," says Tubbs. "I was a late replacement for Tim Witherspoon."

I ask Tubbs about his cultural experience in Tokyo.

"It was a town of little people! I mean, you would go to a club and they had little chairs, little rooms, everything little. But the people were beautiful, and they treated us like royalty.

"Tyson was in another world when he was working with Kevin Rooney and Cus D'Amato. He was the hardest puncher I ever faced, before or since. Tyson was Tyson. He had so much to gain, but the people around him used him and used his name. My fight with him was right at the end of the real Tyson."

He won the fight in the same city where he would lose to Buster Douglas in just under two years. Larry

Merchant gave Tubbs the first round, based on his bodywork and quick hands. Tubbs looked relaxed at the beginning of round 2 and tried to bring his right hand behind the left hook. Tubbs actually landed an uppercut midway through the round that moved Tyson back a bit. However, Tyson would catch up. He would hurt Tubbs badly with a left hook, winning by a 2nd round TKO, registering a sick knockout that had Tubbs lying prone on the canvas and bleeding from the ear. Tyson changed the complexion of the fight in a heartbeat.

"He hit me to the body and then came up and cut me with the left hook. My corner told me to stay down, but a fighter always wants to fight. I feel like I could have gotten up and used my jab to keep him off me. I knew my boxing skills would get me through. His power and speed were devastating, but I was the only one who ever went to the body against him."

Tyson would fight another battle upon his return to New York City, learning that his manager and confidant Jimmy Jacobs had died on March 23, just days after the Tubbs fight. He received the news in the form of a telephone call from Robin Givens, as he was en route to Mt. Sinai Hospital in New York to pay Jacobs a visit.

Jacobs was more than a manager to Tyson—he was one of a handful of surrogate father figures, their relationship forged by a shared passion for boxing and regard for Cus D'Amato. Jacobs, an avid collector of boxing films, often said, "I'm a rich man doing what I'd be doing for nothing."

Jacobs's death, it turned out, left Tyson suscepti-
ble. Indeed, Don King's courtship of the fighter began
at Jacobs's funeral, when, in the lobby of the Beverly
Hilton Hotel, King told the fighter that he didn't have
to go through with the Michael Spinks fight and that
King was offering a five-fight deal worth $5 million.
Jose Torres and Bill Cayton delivered eulogies at the
funeral, and Mike Tyson cried that day.

"Mike did it like he wanted to do it, and he was
both good and evil," remembers Tubbs. "He tells it
like it is. He was a showpiece . . . but I think he just
realized it too late."

In 1989, Tubbs won a decision over Orlin Norris
for the NABF title, but the verdict was later changed
to a no-decision after Tubbs tested positive for an ille-
gal substance.

"I've had a lot of challenges. I was raised in the
church, and I think God has always landed me somewhere to help somebody. I've been able to help people who were down and out . . . give them rides, talk
to them, and keep them out of trouble. I've kept people from shooting people.

"My only regret is that I left Don King . . . I wish
I'd never left him when I was young. I fought Tyson,
originally, to get out of Don's contract. It's like, you
knew he was foul, but you knew you were making
money when you fought for titles, and Don got people title shots. Did you know that Tony Tucker
fought for the title nine times? At the time, if I'd
stayed with Don, I would have made some money.
But I'm trying to make it back now. If I keep up this

winning streak (Tubbs has won three straight come-back fights), you never know."

In what was perhaps the strongest performance of his career, Tubbs fought undefeated prospect Riddick Bowe on March 20, 1991. Utilizing quick hands and a sneaky defense, Tubbs exposed Bowe and lost what many feel was a controversial decision. Ever the enigma, Tubbs lost later to journeyman Lionel Butler but beat future WBA champ Bruce Seldon. Tubbs was inactive from 1998 to 2001. Tubbs lost to rugged veteran Gilbert Mendoza and was stopped by Abraham Okine. However, Tubbs bounced back to earn a victory over undefeated prospect Brian Minto to win the West Virginia heavyweight title.

"If I could crack the top ten and get a shot at one of those guys . . . I may be able to make some decent money and pay off this child support."

Tubbs has fathered between sixteen and twenty children, depending on the source. He is in the precarious place of being a little too dangerous for a real contender—nobody, of course, wanting to lose to a 47-year-old man—but also, realistically, being a little too old and eroded to hang with those fighters. Yet, he fights on.

"That child support is nothing to mess with. They put you in jail for that, you know?"

To say that the ring walk lacks the intensity of a Tyson walk is a vast understatement. We are led out of the small dressing room, past the food prep areas backstage, and through a curtain that opens into the main audience section of the theater. We shimmy around milling fans and past the concession area.

Incidentally, the concession area is manned by a guy in a chef's hat and smock, made to look very gourmet and official. The following is a snippet of dialogue contributed by colleague and *Cincinnati Enquirer* reporter Ryan Ernst:

> **Chef:** *What'll you have?*
> **Ernst:** *What are my options?*
> *(Chef opens catering bin to reveal hot dogs)*
> **Chef:** *Hot dogs.*
> **Ernst:** *I'll have the hot dog.*

Ernst tells the story better than I do, and we laughed about this for a good minute. Welcome to small-time boxing in the Midwest.

Having made our way past the foodservice crowd, we approach the ring. Tubbs's trainer is perturbed that the hanger-on in charge of photographs somehow was left in the back of the large entourage, thus making it impossible for him to snap pictures of Tubbs heading into the ring. Tubbs enters, mostly to curiosity, but to some cheers. This Midwestern fight crowd is as you might expect. There is the right sprinkling of pensioners shuffling around the casino connected to oxygen masks and tough guys who roll up their shirtsleeves and have shaved heads and fat stomachs. Their entire persona seems to scream, "You want a piece of this?" The majority of them, I'm guessing, couldn't fight their way out of a paper bag. Sprinkled into the mix are bored girlfriends who are unimpressed by the spectacle of human violence, and "sponsor" types—that is, local used car salesmen and their girls on the side who ponied up big dollars for a ringside table. Their girls dust off an old bridesmaid dress and dress up for a night at the fights just like the movie starlets in Vegas do on television.

The ring announcer for the evening is former *Playboy* Playmate Amy Hayes. She makes the circuit of Midwestern boxing shows, and I have seen her in places like Grand Rapids, MI, and Merrillville, IN. I feel a very short pang of sadness for her—as the people around me snicker about her physique, about how the faux-tuxedo leotard is a little tighter these days.

Tony Tubbs has made his way into the ring, and I have settled in at ringside, Tubbs's mother behind me, clutching the towel. Even the ring looks old and tired. It lacks the usual advertisements adorning the center of the canvas and the turnbuckle pads. The canvas itself is a muted, filthy blue—made old by years of shuffling shoes, sweat, and blood.

Before the principles are introduced, Aaron "The Hawk" Pryor, a former junior welterweight world champion and Boxing Hall of Famer, steps into the ring and waves. Pryor is exhibit A of a long life lived giving and taking beatings and falling prey to drug abuse. He is a delightful man with charisma who unfortunately sometimes struggles now to communicate. He and his wife, a kind and very sensible-looking woman, now sell memorabilia at these shows—photos and DVDs from Aaron's fights. I will later buy one of his DVDs (his legendary bouts with Alexis Arguello), and he will call Tubbs's comeback a "bad decision."

He saw Tubbs in the gym this week and, quite frankly, wasn't impressed. He remembers Tubbs making his pro debut on one of his undercards twenty-five years ago and doesn't want to see his friend get hurt. He signs my DVD and lets me know that it's still "Hawk Time."

Also not terribly impressive to the eye is Tubbs's opponent Jason Waller. Waller is a pale, pasty 204 pounds and sports boots and trunks that look like they were borrowed from Chuck Wepner. He looks the part of the easy mark, although the fight will prove otherwise.

A slow starter, Waller seems at first to be there just to absorb punishment and go down quickly, his pale, smooth body reddening with welts halfway through the first round. Tubbs's quick punches land at will, at first. But Waller weathers the initial storm, showing a good deal of heart and chin, and begins landing shots of his own as the fight moves into the middle rounds and Tubbs slows considerably.

The rounds themselves seem to last forever. There is nothing quite as painful as watching tired old men fight one another. Their corners douse them with so much water between rounds that the beginning of each subsequent round feels like a swim meet—the water flying off the men with every punch landed. This underscores the image of the slow men punching under water.

"I can't believe they matched him with this guy!" says Tubbs's nervous mother. "They have no business putting him in with a guy 13 years younger!"

I find myself rooting for Waller, not so much out of any affinity for him, but because if Tubbs wins, he will most likely feel compelled to do this again and will one day find himself in with someone much younger who can really hurt him. The nature of boxing journalism is to remain impassive—to not care about the outcome of the fight on a personal level, but to be able to write about what fighters did right or wrong, or simply to recount action. This seems ridiculous to me. What is boxing if not a personal struggle between two people with stories, backgrounds, etc.? The personal stories make the sport rich and also incredibly difficult to watch at times— because nobody likes to see friends take a beating. But if we don't let it become personal, that is, if we just watch fighting for fighting's sake—to win a bet or see blood—it's nothing but a human cockfight, which is infinitely more depressing.

Waller is relative baby at 34 years old. Forty-seven-year-old heavyweights are hard to come by in the Midwest, or pretty much anywhere else.

"Next time you should train more than ten days!" she yells to her son in the ring. Family at ringside is a curious sight at most boxing shows. Bringing mom to a casino, a club, or at best an arena to watch you take (or at best give) a beating seems counterintuitive.

Tubbs is slowing considerably. Both men being exhausted, neither does any real damage, but Waller seems to be hell-bent on coming forward. He absorbs three shots for every one he lands, and Tubbs's quick hands are slowed by a lack of conditioning. There are moments in which it looks like Tubbs will lose. It seems like the man who runs out of gas last will win.

The end comes for Waller in the seventh, as he, quite simply, is exhausted. There is a distinct moment in most pro fights in which the other man loses his spirit—the point where he realizes he can't win, and that it's only a matter of time before he loses a decision or is concussed. Call it the moment of truth or whatever—it doesn't really matter. He gets floored by a legitimate Tubbs right hand and takes an eight-count, and then takes two successive standing eights, resulting in a three-knockdown-rule TKO victory for Tubbs. Waller's facial expression never changed from start to finish; he was a man doing a job and he did it well. He almost finished it off, which would have been a great story to tell the boys back at work. Waller walks to his dressing room alone, having borrowed a corner man for the evening from one of the other fighters. He sits by himself on the pleather sofa, completely exhausted. One by one the other fighters from the card line up and come into the small room to give their congratulations on a fight well fought, to a guy that flew in this afternoon by himself.

The Tubbs dressing room, on the other hand, is buoyant. There is nothing in sports like a winning locker room. Even though all in attendance would agree (but wouldn't say) that he looked less than impressive, there is talk of future fights.

"I knew how to win the rounds," says Tubbs. "I would throw combinations toward the end of the rounds until he started showing me his chin."

He is asked about what he learned tonight.

"To move up I have to bring in good sparring partners and do this right. Basically, all I did before this fight was hit the heavy bag and the speed bag. When you do that you get a little glove-shy and you don't get your timing right. But this fight showed me I still have speed."

Unfortunately, he will do this again. Calkins is making plans for a September date in Iowa.

"The conditioning was there," Tubbs continues. "But that was a real fight—it was a seven-round 'who-gonna-do-what-to-who.'"

The assembled hangers-on, myself included, do what good hangers-on do and laugh. Tubbs is high on the win. A member of the entourage brings a plate of hot dogs for the triumphant fighter.

"I didn't see many empty seats in there," Tubbs reflects. "Did that room look sold out to ya'all?!"

There is an Elvis impersonator playing in the Grand Victoria lounge, adjacent to the ballroom, where patrons are flowing out into the night. I see many familiar faces as I walk past the lounge, the sounds of bad music and laughter spilling into the hallway. I would walk the halls a little bit later, unable to sleep, winding my way out past the ice machines and the concierge desk. I would approach Tubbs, now alone, wearing a pair of sweats and a jacket—all of the well-wishers have left for the evening, off to slot machines or rest. I catch his eye and nod, telling him "good fight" one last time.

SECONDS OUT

THE PETER McNEELY **INTERLUDE**

PETER McNEELY IS A GUY that you root for, really for no good reason. You dial his number, not expecting to get him, but he answers and tells you stories . . . about his dad hanging out with James Caan and George Perles in college. About how he just bought his first home with some of the money left over from the Tyson fight. Peter McNeely is endearing because he is one of us. A guy trying to make ends meet. He was tongue-in-cheek about his fame even when he was famous for 15 minutes.

"I'm doing labor and shit now," he says, with no sense of irony or humor. "I'm not technically retired yet. I haven't fought in four years, but I've been on call for the last seven or eight years taking fights on short notice. I need a couple of quick wins to get back into the money fights."

You agree to meet at a gym on Saturday, but you hang up the phone feeling sad, because you know those money fights will never come.

THE ENDURING IMAGE of "Hurricane" Peter Mc-Neely is that of the Boston club fighter being knocked out by a pizza crust. McNeely, like all good businessmen (and many of Tyson's previous opponents), knew his time in the spotlight was short and that the 15 minutes of fame go pretty fast and are capable of generating much revenue.

McNeely, however, turned out to be the perfect sales tool for Tyson's first post-prison ring appearance. McNeely was a throwback—a white "dem and doze" East Coaster with a dad who fought and a well-documented drinking problem. McNeely also had a generous dose of what many pro fighters do not—charisma. He was an honest and genuine interview in a sports climate of cliches and meaningless talk. People, myself included, simply liked him.

He had a certain deer-in-headlights look before the Tyson bout, a look that gave you the same feeling you got when the weaker kid got beat up on the playground but took it like a man. Some weird combination of pity and respect. Tyson was shredded and looked stone cold across the ring. Cut, with prison tats and a bored expression. The whole world knew this was going to be ugly, but how ugly and for how long was the question.

At the bell McNeely charged across the ring like a bull and was promptly deposited on his backside. He popped up immediately and began jogging around the ring. You knew you were watching a guy who was severely outclassed, but also a guy who liked fighting and wanted to be there. That, at least, made things interesting.

PETER McNEELEY'S MANAGER, Vinny Vecchione, has just hung up the telephone after telling me, in no uncertain terms, that Peter McNeeley will not be meeting with me in Boston. I have that feeling that people get when they're so close to making something happen without getting caught. I was looking forward to an hour or so of Peter's stories, of good banter without a manager digging into my wallet or looking over my shoulder. Not to be.

Vecchione seemed genuinely upset to be talking to me. Upset at the audacity of requesting an interview with his fighter without paying both of them large sums of money. "Let's talk," he said, when I picked up the phone. I launched into my spiel about the book, about wanting to do a chapter on Peter. "No, let's talk terms." Terms? Besides you and your fighter getting to feel famous one more time? I explained that in journalism it wasn't standard to pay for interviews and that nobody involved in this project would be getting rich. In fact, all of my advance (and then some) has already gone into the coffers of Delta, Northwest, and American Airlines. I wasn't about to pay these guys. I told Vecchione that there would be no money, only an opportunity to discuss Peter, his career, his legacy, and what it was like to be in the ring with Tyson.

"Thank you very much," he said. And hung up the telephone.

CHAPTER TEN

BUSTER **MATHIS JR.**

*I believe nature's a lot smarter than any man
thinks. During the course of a man's life, he
develops a lot of pleasures and people he cares
about. And then nature takes them away, one by
one. It's her way of preparing you for death.*

—CUS D'AMATO

A FEW NOTEWORTHY ITEMS of trivia regarding
Buster Mathis Jr.'s fight with Mike Tyson on December 16, 1995, in Philadelphia: The fight aired on live,
free television (the Fox Network) and set their all-
time Neilsen ratings record. Buster Mathis had
$4,000 in cash (to pay sparring partners) stolen from
his hotel room at the Philadelphia Marriot on the
night of the fight. "I had it hidden in my pants pocket
and stuffed in my suitcase—whoever found that must
have been a professional." The thief used a room key
to enter the room and take the cash, and due to a
loophole in the Pennsylvania Innkeeper's Act, the

Mathis camp was not eligible for remuneration. And finally, after knocking Mathis out in the 3rd round, Tyson hugged him and whispered in his ear, "You know, we're still brothers."

"I knew Tyson before we fought," says Mathis, who is squeezed into a booth at the New Beginnings Restaurant in Kentwood, MI. He and his matchmaker Bruce Kielty (business card says "man-about-boxing") have agreed to meet me for lunch. And in spite of their careers spent largely in boxing, the two are remarkably normal, even nice. Mathis, 35, looks to be right around his fighting weight of 225 and is dressed in a sharp suede sportcoat. Kielty is on his way to work as an administrator at a Grand Rapids mental hospital and is dressed accordingly.

"I never made boxing a career," he says. "A lot of matchmakers put their guys in whenever their daughters needed braces or another tuition payment . . . but at the end I got offers for fights that I didn't even tell Buster about."

"I hope you didn't get any million-dollar offers," says Buster, in his distinctively high voice. The two laugh; clearly they have rapport.

Mathis fought a very reasonable 26 fights and is noticeably uncompromised by the sport, physically. His voice is clear, strong, and discernable. This is a function of both his short career and his slipping, defensive style taught by his father, also a protege of Cus D'Amato.

"I think the method is what made Tyson special. I think if Tyson went back to the method-is-madness, fear-is-your-friend mentality in the Catskills, he would have a couple more years and a few more good fights in him. Maybe to not make the heavyweight championship of the world, but to make some good money and retire from the game. If Kevin Rooney cleaned up his act, he could work with Kevin again. Kevin didn't take any BS from Mike, and Kevin genuinely cared about him. The things he gets away with with other trainers, he couldn't get away with with Kevin. Other trainers just care about the money, about the 10 percent they were going to get from Mike. He was no more than a paycheck. With Kevin, Mike had to be in bed at a certain time. And Mike needs to get back to working the Willie every day."

At this point Kielty interjects, interpreting my confused look. "Explain the Willie, Bus."

"I worked the Willie every day," he says. "It's a stationary heavybag that is attached to the floor. D'Amato and Rooney had a numbering system for all of their punches. If you watch Tyson's old fights you can hear them shouting numbers from the corner. One, two, five! And so forth. This is the code. These numbers signify the punches that a fighter would throw in the fight, so you work the Willie to work on these combinations. I believe in the Willie. Kevin Rooney believes in the Willie. Steve Lott believes in the Willie. When I look at Mike's fights today, it's clear to me that he's not working the Willie. Mike got away from that, you know what I'm saying? I think that if Mike got back to that Willie situation then he would be a much better fighter than he is right now."

"He's a straight-up slugger now," says Kielty. "He's ordinary."

Mathis speaks of the "Willie situation" with an almost religious fervor. The Willie was, in fact, originally called the "Willie Bag" in honor of Willie Pastrano, from whom D'Amato protege Jose Torres would win the light heavyweight title. It was comprised simply of five matresses wrapped around a frame, on the front of which was drawn the rough outline of a man's body. Number 1 was a left hook to the jaw, number 2 a right hook to the jaw, number 3 a left uppercut, number 4 a right uppercut, number 5 a left hook to the body, number 6 a right hook to the body, number 7 a jab to the head, and number 8 a jab to the body. For D'Amato proteges, there was also the sand-filled "slip" bag, a tear-shaped black bag about the size of a fist that would swing from a length of rope. Fighters would move side to side and dip down, just as they would to avoid actual punches.

"Mike was hell on wheels in those days," he says. "But I always knew I would fight Mike Tyson. That was my plan—get in, win some fights, fight Mike, and get out. My goal wasn't the heavyweight title, it was to make some money fighting Tyson and then get on with my life. Boxing was a means to an end."

Despite his father's presence in his life, Mathis's route to a boxing career was less than direct. He found the sport as a 300-pound teenager who had failed at his other athletic endeavors.

"I had tried other sports . . . football and basketball," he recalls, "but boxing was the only sport that ever accepted me. A lot of the other sports, like football or track, I quit."

"My father didn't want me to box," says Mathis. "He said no, no, no, because he thought I was just going to quit. I never saw his films or memorabilia. So for about a year we went to the gym together before it opened and my father trained me. My dad and I were close—we were best friends. We always spent the time before and after the workouts talking."

What did you talk about, I wondered.

"We talked about boxing and business. We discussed strategy. How I would use boxing to make a name for myself and then get out of the business and move on to other things, which is exactly what my dad did. My dad had dyslexia," he says, "but he worked and he didn't just live off his name. He went to work every morning for Interstate Trucking Company."

"After Buster lost 100 pounds, his dad came to me and said 'I think Buster is ready for a fight,'" says Kielty. "I wasn't terribly convinced. I told his dad that sometimes skills don't pass down through the genes—I wasn't sure boxing was going to be a fit for Buster. Bus was a heavyset guy and was very laid back, but he was developing the beginnings of a style predicated on head slips and aggression. So I found him a 40-year-old amateur guy from Lansing for his first fight. We put him on a card at the Playboy Club down there."

Mathis won that fight, and many others. After a distinguished amateur career, including a victory in the Michigan Golden Gloves, Mathis finally began to feel the success—both athletically and socially—that had eluded him before.

"I remember after the [Golden] Gloves," he recalls. "Bruce showed me that there was an article written about me in a paper in Japan. Japan! The idea that people halfway across the world were reading about me really changed my life. The fact that I won the state championship and my name was being read in Japan. I took that paper to school and showed everybody that they were writing about me in Japan! I think that was the turning point for me."

"Bus was an introvert before he started boxing," says Kielty.

Mathis fought on, compiling a professional record of 20–0 and a world ranking of number 4 by the IBF, before facing Tyson. His resume included a victory over fringe contender Mike "The Bounty" Hunter.

"I knew Tyson before that," he says. "Once, when I was 14, Mike was fighting a guy [Jesse Ferguson] in Detroit. My dad had heard that he was partying a lot, hanging out, and wasn't taking his training seriously. So Dad called him up and said, 'What the hell are you doing?' Basically chewed him out and said that he should be at home focusing on the fight. Dad was a part of the D'Amato family . . . it was like a tight niche up in New York with Jim Jacobs, Steve Lott, and Jose Torres. That Cus D'Amato thing is like a family.

"Anyway, Dad puts me on the phone with Tyson, who wasn't champ yet but was already a millionaire and was tearing through the division. I was 14 years old and had never fought a day in my life. I told Mike, 'One day I'm going to fight you.' All he said was, 'Kid, listen to your father, he's a helluva guy.' That's the only thing he said. That's what I was training for, not to become heavyweight champion of the world, but to fight Tyson, get the money, and haul ass. It's like every era has its guy—in the 40s it was Joe Louis, in my dad's era it was Muhammad Ali, and in my era it was Mike Tyson. When you fight those guys, it's an opportunity to make a name for yourself. Think about it, out of all the people in Grand Rapids, I'm the only one who's fought Mike Tyson."

THERE ARE OTHER THINGS you should know about Buster Mathis, Jr. He is close to receiving his degree in sports management from the University of Miami. His middle name is D'Amato. He only fought 26 times and retired once, at age 26. And his father died six weeks before his first scheduled fight with Mike Tyson.

"Tyson knew the situation and his camp claimed injury," says Kielty, "to give us time to find another trainer and reschedule the fight."

The Tyson camp claimed an injured hand, and rumors abound as to the validity of the claim. Some even say that the Tyson camp showed Shaquille O'Neal's X-rays (the big center, who was then struggling with a broken hand) to the media. At any rate, the fight was rescheduled and moved, from Las Vegas to the Spectrum in Philadelphia. Mathis would eventually hire trainer Joey Fariello, another D'Amato disciple.

"I knew the D'Amato code, like Mike did," says Mathis. "People asked him before the fight if he was worried about fighting a guy trained in the method . . . worried that I was working with Fariello. And Mike said, 'I'm not fighting Joe Fariello.'"

"I was unlike most guys, in that I wasn't at all afraid of Mike—I knew him. When I fought Riddick Bowe? Yeah, I was nervous. That's a large man with power. Mike was small . . . you really get the feel for what a tiny guy he is when you're with him. But with Mike, it wasn't so much the power that got you, but the speed. He was lighting fast . . . moved like a middleweight in there.

"In fact, and I don't think I've even told Bruce this, I went to Mike's hotel room the night before the fight. I went up there just to see how he was doing, because without the entourages around I could talk to Mike just like I'm talking to you. There was a security guy outside his door, and I told him I was Buster and he let me in. We just chatted for a few minutes. Mike wished me luck and told me to enjoy myself. And he told me again how much he liked my father. He was cool. Nice guy, helluva guy. When I got back downstairs Joey [Fariello] said, 'Bus, what the hell are you thinking?' I said, 'I just went up to say nice fight,' and he said, 'Don't ever do that again!'"

"You learn something new every day," says Kielty. "By and large, our relationship with Tyson was cordial the whole time. But he became a different person when Don King and his entourage were around. He was different around Rory Holloway, John Horne, and . . . who was the guy that was always jumping around yelling?"

Panama Lewis.

"Yeah, 'The Court Jester,'" says Kielty.

"Mike got a little upset with me at the weigh-in," Mathis recalls. "I was laughing to myself during the staredown, because I couldn't get over what a small guy he was. I said to myself, 'How in the hell can a guy who's this tiny generate so much power?' This is going through my mind. Mike took my laughing as an insult. He said, 'You better show up tomorrow night.'"

MATHIS DID SHOW UP, even though he did so for a fraction of the negotiated purse.

"You could write an entire book about the time leading up to the Tyson fight, but none of us want to relive that again," says Kielty. "We had Buster's dad die as we were getting ready to sign for the Tyson fight, we had to replace Buster's manager, and then Buster's trainer Joe Fariello died ten days after the fight."

The Mathis camp won a lawsuit against a man acting as Mathis's manager, who actually falsified his identity while he was working with the fighter. They won the suit in 2002 but still have yet to be paid.

"It would have to be a comedy type of thing to laugh at this stuff," adds Mathis, half-joking. "A lot of fighters, believe it or not, have been through stuff like this."

"We ended up suing Buster's manager and promoter in two massive lawsuits in New York federal court and won both cases," Kielty recalls. "The legal hassles in boxing are worse than the fights themselves."

The title of the promotion was "Presumption of Innocence," more a tongue-in-cheek nod to Don King's legal troubles at the time than to any in-fight storyline.

Kielty was summoned to the room of promoter Cedric Kushner the evening before the fight. There was a crisis afoot, he was told, and purse renegotiations were in order.

"Kushner basically said that the promotion was hurting, and that we needed to renegotiate Buster's purse. He said that Mike Tyson had already agreed to take a cut in his purse from $10 million down to $5 million, and that Paul Vaden and Terry Norris, the cofeature fighters, had also taken cuts. So I talked to Joey [Fariello] and he said, 'If you want to walk right now, I can be packed in an hour.' He was ready to walk. When I saw Buster, I said, 'You're going to have to make a decision on what you're going to do.' He said, 'What would you do?' He said, 'It makes me mad, but I'll take the fight.' So ultimately we ended up fighting."

As financial records would later (two years later) indicate, they were the only camp on the card to fight for a pay cut. Vaden, Norris, and Tyson were all paid in full. This after another protracted lawsuit involving Mathis Jr.'s manager at the time, who, as it turned out, was a con man operating under an assumed identity and had allegedly negotiated the fight as a result of a bribe. Such is the messy world of big-time boxing.

"I had never in my life sued anyone or been sued," says Kielty. "Needless to say, this was an eye-opener."

The fight itself was an eye-opener for those who expected the fleshy Mathis to provide a stationary target for a Tyson who at this stage in his career was trading the D'Amato style for that of the slugger. Mathis proved to be an awkward, relaxed opponent, and hard to hit.

"I remember Joey telling Bus that if you can feel your nose hairs pull away from Tyson's chest hairs, you're too far away from him," recalls Kielty. "And Buster wasn't afraid; in fact, he took a nap in the dressing room about 30 minutes before the fight."

Mathis charged across the ring at the opening bell and immediately set up shop on Mike Tyson's chest. Through subtle slips and head movements, he avoided Tyson's bombs, causing him to miss wildly, much to the dismay of the crowd. As for Tyson, he had a look of relaxed detachment on his face during the fight. He looked more like a man trying to figure out a jigsaw puzzle or put together a model airplane while on holiday than a cold-blooded killer. He knew that Mathis's power provided no threat and that it was just a matter of time before he figured out the angles and completed the puzzle.

Mathis survived, for roughly eight minutes. He slipped and flurried, moving subtly around the ring on a giant set of legs—indeed his ankles and thighs seemed to be one. Not the body one imagines on a world-class athlete, but effective nonetheless. Mathis was given a great deal of credit for lasting into the 3rd round.

"I knew when Mike was going to catch me," Mathis recalls. "I slipped the wrong way and knew that it was coming."

MATHIS WAS KNOCKED OUT with about a minute remaining in the 3rd round. A calm, collected Tyson then gave a surreal post-fight interview with his daughter sitting on his lap. Tyson reasserted that nobody knew "the style" better than he did, and that he kept good on his promise to give the people of Philadelphia something to remember. It was as content as he had looked in a long time.

"I'm very familiar with his style of fighting," said Tyson after the fight, "and I'm the best at that style of fighting . . . I really didn't hit him as hard as I anticipated, but I knew the punches would hurt him because he didn't see them coming . . . I'm just looking forward to doing well and I don't care who it is [I'm fighting]."

As for Mathis, he returned to the Philadelphia Marriot to find his room ransacked—as were the rooms of several members of his camp. A less than ceremonious end to a fight that launched the first day of the rest of Buster Mathis Jr.'s life. Tyson, meanwhile, was beginning to be exposed as a slugger and would fight on through the end of the decade and beyond.

"My goal was to fight Mike Tyson and get out of there," says Mathis. "Every era has a guy . . . and for our era it was Tyson."

"Mike's name is still worth a million bucks," he continues. "He should go into promotion. Start his own promotional company. He can have more influence on the business side of the sport now, if he surrounds himself with good people and, like De La Hoya, can start to move more of the dishonest elements out of the sport."

Mathis would be interested in being a part of such a venture, he says. He has also dabbled in training fighters and would like to be a part of sharing the D'Amato method with another generation of boxers, such as Nigerian prospect Sam Peter, who has been compared, at least in build and power-potential, with Tyson. Mathis is also an aspiring screenwriter, having written a couple of screenplays and submitted treatments to PBS for an interview program, and has a certificate in real estate development from USC.

I ask, finally, about his impressions of Tyson, the person.

"The last time I talked with Mike was when Floyd Mayweather fought Henry Bruseles . . . When people talk about Mike's childhood and his upbringing, they don't understand that he was adopted by Cus and Camille and basically grew up in a mansion. He had it tough up to a certain point, but after that he was a prodigy and was treated like one. He was a multimillionaire by the time he was nineteen and a half years old."

"I think most of the negative stuff started after Jimmy Jacobs passed away," says Kielty. "Jacobs was the guy with the most influence on Mike publicly, and he was just a very good businessman. I remember an instance where I had done a favor for Jim, and he was very appreciative—as I recall, it had to do with helping him find a fight film that he had lost. At any rate, he flew me down to Las Vegas for the Pinklon Thomas fight and there were two front row seats laying on the sofa in my hotel room."

"You went to that fight?" Mathis interjects. "Was it awesome?"

I HAVE ASKED THE TWO why Buster made a clear and final decision to leave the sport when so many of his contemporaries retired and unretired whenever their whims or financial needs dictated.

"Sometimes I just like to put the boxing stuff behind me," he says. "Once I retired from boxing, I never looked back. If I die, I don't want to be known as the guy who fought Mike Tyson, I want to be known as the guy who built a skyscraper or the guy who ran for Congress. I like politics . . . I like John McCain and Rudy Guiliani, I think they could be a helluva team together."

"I think the business of boxing became distasteful to Buster," says Kielty. "I don't think he lost his taste for boxing so much as the business of boxing.

"We had offers to fight in Europe . . . we could have made $20,000 to $30,000 at a time, but it just wasn't worth risking Buster's health. Like everyone else in boxing, we tried to send some e-mails and faxes to George Foreman, but George didn't want to fight somebody that moved his head like Buster."

"You gotta know when to hold 'em, know when to fold 'em, know when to walk away, and know when to run," says Mathis, invoking Kenny Rodgers.

"I remember watching Buster warm up for his last fight against Lou Savarese. He was warming up in a tent outside the venue and as our cut man watched him, he said, 'Buster's lost his edge hasn't he?' That was our last fight."

I ask Mathis what changed for him, and why the sport no longer held its appeal.

"It lost its appeal when I lost my father. The only joy in winning was sharing it with him. I tried to share it with Kevin Rooney, but it never really worked out.

My mom never believed in fighting and never came to see me fight, even though she supported me. With her it was always, 'Bus, you need to come back to Kingdom Hall!' But boxing was something I shared with Dad. People grieve when they lose their fathers, but when you lose your best friend, you hurt for a long time. Dad was my best friend."

CHAPTER ELEVEN

EVANDER **HOLYFIELD**

When you conceal your will from others, that is
Thick. When you impose your will on others, that
is Black.

—LEE ZHONG WU, *THICK FACE, BLACK HEART*

IT'S 11:48 A.M., and I fear that I am about to conduct the world's most expensive phone interview. I
flew into Atlanta this morning and rented a car, winding my way out from Hartsfield Airport and down
Old National Highway, which, for about a half a
mile in front of his sprawling, palatial, (insert
grandiose adjective here) estate, becomes Evander
Holyfield Highway.

"I'm Ted Kluck, with the *Facing Tyson* project,
I'm here to interview Mr. Holyfield." And yes, if
you're wondering, calling him Mr. Holyfield feels a
little ridiculous, but everybody here calls him Mr.
Holyfield, so I follow suit.

"Mr. Holyfield is in Cancun," says the guy at the
gate. I ask him to repeat himself because it's a little

windy out and I thought I just heard him say that Mr. Holyfield is in Cancun. My flight out leaves at 5:30. I confirmed this appointment yesterday. I can feel my blood pressure skyrocket, and wonder for a moment what it would be like to have a stroke at Disney Field. Guy at Gate goes back inside to make some calls on my behalf. I take the opportunity to peer through the gate, emblazoned with the Team Holyfield logo. The wrought iron fence—more of a metal wall—stretches for about 400 meters in both directions. There are ducks. I think I see some horse barns. The usual rich guy stuff. If this were a documentary, this is where we would put the walk and talk through the horse stables. But it isn't. It's me getting shafted out of another interview, which could very well be the alternate title for this book.

"He's expected in sometime today," says Guy at Gate, who I notice has a nice selection of DVDs to keep him occupied while he guards The Fortress. "And we can't let you in to wait inside because it's not on his calendar. In fact, nobody knows about it."

I envision a day inside my rented, midsize Chevy Cobalt and wheel my car out of the complex in search of a giant chain bookstore in which to camp for the next six hours, looking over my right shoulder at a house roughly the size of a college dormitory, with Evander Holyfield nowhere to be found.

JOHN HORNE IS GOING CRAZY. Horne, you'll recall, was a part of Tyson's "management" during the dark period—the years after prison, when he was spending wildly (How do you go broke on $100 million? Spend $105 million.), looking ordinary in the ring, and finally, biting ears. Horne was the tall, skinny one—part of a "Mutt and Jeff" inseparable combination with the shorter, pudgier Rory Holloway. Think of them as Don King's interns.

Horne is screaming at distinguished reporter Jim Gray, who, in addition to insightful, professional work, also has a real knack for exasperating people. Horne is describing the bite that his client took out of Evander Holyfield's ear as "a nip," while describing Tyson's own cut as a "three-inch gash" over his right eye. He yells this in Gray's direction while looking off somewhere into space, as if he is too angry to even look at the little reporter. He explains, in his own logic, that Tyson was justified in "taking a nip" out of Holyfield's ear—a ghastly nip that lay on the canvas at the MGM Grand—and that the fight should have continued. He cited Holyfield's repeated head butts ("One head butt may be accidental, fifteen is not!") and low blows—all true—but failed to mention that his man was being soundly beaten and his mounting frustration resulted in the L, DQ 3 in the record books. "He [Holyfield] jumped around like a little bitch," adds Horne, as if there is some other common reaction to having a chunk of one's ear bitten off. "He [Holyfield] turned it into a street fight a long time ago."

Horne's interview seems to never end, and at some point the screaming gave way to a calm, rational Don King. King explains that something should have been done about the head butts, but that the proper reaction is indeed not to bite. "Boxing is unpredictable," says King, "that's what makes it so great." This is King playing the part of the quiet church mouse—promising to seek justice and, above all, pay his fighters. This is what makes King a legendary huckster-prince and Horne, now in 2006, anonymous.

"We're in a fight already," said Holyfield after the fight. "So if you feel like you can whup me, why didn't you whup me with the gloves on . . . this is a boxing match . . . this is not when the fight gets over you get brave and then you want to fight."

Only in America.

"What am I to do?" asked Tyson post-fight. "This is my career, I can't keep getting butted like that . . . I've got children to raise . . . Listen, Holyfield's not the tough warrior that everyone says he is . . . he's got a little nick on his ear . . . I've got one eye! If he takes one, I've got another one, I'm ready to fight. I'm ready to fight right now . . . I've gotta go home to my kids, look at me."

FAST FORWARD TO the present day—the day where I am driving around aimlessly in Fayetteville, GA, and finally get a call from Mr. Holyfield's person (Meka, thank you again for your hard work) that Mr. Holyfield was indeed back and willing to see me.

In real life, Holyfield actually looks a little taller than he does on tape. I'm six feet two inches, and he actually felt a little taller, although it could have just been a combination of the vast, Ecclesiastical riches, the fame, and the fact that people call him "Mr." I feel about five feet three inches by comparison.

At any rate, Holyfield looks and sounds fit. There has been much debate recently about his condition (word slurring, etc.) on Internet message boards, but to my untrained medical eye he seems the picture of health. It is this health, he says, that will allow him to win another world championship, his fourth time—one more than Ali, he is quick to point out. He makes it clear that this, the positive—the idea of a next title—is what we will be discussing this evening. (A note about Holyfield's study, which is where we're chatting. It's huge. It looks like the office you imagine having as a kid, when you imagine that you're unbelievably rich and you have a giant office, where you sit in a velvet robe and smoke cigars, dreaming of your next conquest. There are original paintings of Holyfield in here, gloves signed by Ali, a fireplace, lots of leather chairs, and a random collection of boxing books. It's a sweet room.)

Evander Holyfield is animated. He often stands up from the small table and walks around the room as he makes points. At times he bounces up and assumes the fighter's stance—hands up, flicking imaginary punches into the air, his gold Holyfield Records medallion swinging around his muscular neck with each punch. I feel an odd sort of sympathy for him. This is a man who loves fighting more than anything, but soon won't be able to do it anymore.

"My goal is to be heavyweight champ again," he continues. "I would like to break George's [Foreman] record. Right now I feel that I'm a light—a light that's there to give people a chance to see that they can do things they set out to do. I tell people who doubt me—all the writers and boxing people—that they all underestimate the power of knowledge. None of the other fighters, including Ali, took care of themselves the way that I do. I'm 43, and it will probably be another year or so before I fight for the title, so that's realistic."

The realistic-ness of this comment is also the subject of much debate in the boxing community, as Holyfield is having trouble getting licensed to fight in the United States based on his poor performances against Chris Byrd, James Toney, and Larry Donald, respectively. He is even quick to admit that these were indeed bad performances, but also adds that he has had operations on his shoulder since then and feels better than ever in the gym. I ask Evander Holyfield about his health. About the accumulation of punches taken over a lifetime of boxing.

"I don't worry about health because I do the right things. I take care of myself and my body. There are so many people in boxing who don't. There are too many people in this sport that care more about drinking and partying than about taking care of themselves. It's all about the choices we make."

I am trying, in vain, to turn our conversation to his two victories over Mike Tyson. I am trying to talk about the past, while Evander Holyfield seems set on talking about the future.

"I don't have any animosity toward Tyson about our second fight," he says. The fight, of course, where Tyson made dubious boxing and cultural history by taking two rather large chunks out of Evander Holyfield's right ear at the MGM Grand Garden Arena in Las Vegas, before being disqualified by referee Mills Lane. In spite of the good work of plastic surgeons, one can see that Holyfield's right ear is still somewhat misshapen by the incident. The word "pandemonium" doesn't adequately describe the circus that went down that evening. It can be summarized as follows: Tyson is cut because of an inadvertent head butt (which Tyson thought was intentional), Tyson complains repeatedly to Mills Lane before taking matters into his own hands by gnoshing on Holyfield's now famous ear. Tyson is disqualified after, incredibly, the fight is allowed to go on after the first bite (Lane wanted to stop it, but Nevada Boxing Commissioner Marc Ratner overruled by asking, "Do you really want to stop this fight?," stopping short of adding, "in front of all these people?") Post-fight, Tyson charges across the ring, swinging at security, trying to work his way toward an astonished Holyfield. The lackeys posture and shove. It is a melee and now a piece of pop-culture infamy.

"I've seen Tyson several times since, and we were just like, 'Hey, what's up?' You know, it's easy to forgive Mike Tyson, because I'm not a perfect person either. I have forgiven him in my heart."

I ask him about his mind-set going into the two fights. Holyfield was the rare Tyson opponent who didn't seem visibly shaken by the idea of fighting him. The Holyfield who entered that ring in the MGM Grand was a relative Cool Hand Luke. Fearless. Tyson, by comparison, was the one who was unable to make eye contact during the pre-fight instructions and stare down in their second fight.

"It was like this. Today is the day where the two best fighters fight. And you know what? One person can only occupy the position. And we're trying to get to the same place at the same time. This man [Tyson] had been in that place for a long time and now it was time for me to be in that place. It's like trying to be the president of a company. Both of ya'all can't be it. That's why they have a vice president.

"I used Tyson as an inspiration and as a motivator because he was a small heavyweight who fought huge guys—guys six feet five inches and 240—but he never complained. He just beat the dog out of them. He never said, 'My arms are too short.'

"The whole thing with a bully is to say, 'I know you hit hard—I'm going to take your best shot and then I'm going to hit you back.' He wasn't accustomed to it. With Mike, I tried to hit him two or three shots for every shot of his that I took. Bap. Bap. Bap. I gotta get mad and move. It's a thinking game. I want to make a person feel like they're sorry for ever getting in the ring with me."

Holyfield is up out of his seat again, gliding over the hardwood floors in his Prada shoes, showing me the techniques and the spatial relationships he used to keep Tyson at bay.

"My thing was to get myself in a position, right, and then say to the other guy, you're not going to stop me from getting to my position. I've got to figure out how to get there, because if I don't get there, I can't win. You're not going to back me down. I'm gonna hurt you too, so what you gonna do? You're a man just like me. I trained for it and you trained for it."

Holyfield is out of the chair again now, whipping imaginary punches against the air as he explains these principles.

"And I'm not going to let fear stop me from getting into position either. The Bible said, 'Fear not what can hurt your body, as long as it can't touch your soul.' I'll make you fight my kind of fight."

Holyfield controlled Tyson in their first bout, on November 9, 1996, by employing a mix of power punches, combinations, and an outright refusal to be backed down or intimidated. Both men needed the fight for essentially the same reason. While Tyson was away (imprisoned), Holyfield came in and set up residence in his house (the heavyweight division). Holyfield, the ultimate competitor, needed to beat Tyson to regain the titles and gain the satisfaction that comes from beating the best. Tyson needed the same thing. It had been a long time since Tyson had beaten anyone good (Donovan Ruddock, 1991) and, in retrospect, that Ruddock fight would be his last significant win. The result was a truly epic heavyweight fight between two active, well-conditioned fighters, with Holyfield ultimately scoring a TKO in the 11th round to regain the WBA heavyweight crown. His refusal to be outworked and outconditioned contributed greatly to the win, in a fight named the 1996 Fight of the Year and Upset of the Year by *Ring Magazine*. Tyson, however, showed courage in defeat, as he would later against Lennox Lewis—something that was absent in their second fight, a fight which could have been equally great but ended, on June 28 of 1997, in infamy. Tyson was breathing heavily and looked visibly exhausted by the 10th round in their first bout, a weakness which rarely appeared during the first (pre-prison) portion of Tyson's career. In the

11th, after a furious Holyfield flurry which Tyson couldn't return, referee Mitch Halpern stepped in between the two fighters as bedlam erupted in the ring. Holyfield was lifted above the throng by his supporters while Tyson slunk back to his corner, defeated. He bowed his head while the throng swirled around him. The MGM Grand crowd roared its approval.

"My God is the only true God," said Holyfield in a post-fight interview with Ferdie Pacheco. "Everything must bow to the true God."

"Let's get off religion," said Ferdie Pacheco, "and talk boxing. How did you fight such a brilliant fight?"

"I was led by the spirit of God," replied Holyfield, "and whatever the spirit tells me to do, that's what I do. Everybody thought that I was washed up, but with God I'm not washed up . . . it wasn't about being tired at the end, it was about what the Lord wanted me to do."

The Lord, apparently, wanted him to beat up Mike Tyson. The Tyson camp complained of head butts throughout, but referee Mitch Halpern explained that the two that he called were, in fact, accidental.

"Both guys led with their heads," said Halpern. "That's just their style and that's how they fought. It wasn't a dirty thing, they would just lay their heads on each other and there was no intentional butting here at all . . . you've got two big guys and two great fighters."

Tyson appeared dazed and winded in his post-fight interview. He is asked what happened.

"I wasn't really aware of what happened, I'd have to review the tapes to really assess what happened," he replied and then added, softly, "He fought a good fight."

As was the case with nearly every fighter who beat Tyson, the two fights were something of career-definers for Holyfield, who would go on to beat Michael Moorer and John Ruiz for heavyweight titles in wins that paled in comparison to his bouts with Tyson and three epic wars with Riddick Bowe, which produced some of the best rounds in heavyweight boxing history.

EVANDER HOLYFIELD LIKES talking about success. He was born in 1962, in Altmore, Alabama, the ninth child of a lumberjack and a cook, and spent most of his young life in the projects of Atlanta. He learned his legendary work ethic, he says, from his parents.

"One of the strangest things about growing up in the projects was all of the sexual stuff. I remember I had just turned 18 and there was this one strip club in the neighborhood that for years I had wanted to go to. I had always tried to get in when I was a kid, and when I turned 18, I finally got to go in and I took my seat in the front row. I was sitting there watching the girls dance and this older guy sat down next to me and he turned to me and said, 'Son, when I was your age I wouldn't be in here lookin' at these girls, I'd be havin' me one.'"

There is a moral in this story, I know. Holyfield fills the awkward silence.

"What he was trying to say was that I should be out getting to know girls—conversing with them—

instead of sitting in here. From that point on, I never went to a strip club."

Evander Holyfield's stories offer very little in the way of ambiguity. There is always a moral to be learned. I learn that his kids aren't allowed to have pop or candy in the house, because their health and self-discipline are very important to him, and because he didn't have candy as a child. That he missed proms and dances in high school so that he could train. That his mom taught him to be courteous and never wear his feelings on his sleeve. That growing up poor filled him with an almost insatiable desire to succeed and prove himself. That life is all about choices, and successful people choose to overcome boredom. And that almost everywhere he goes, as a successful person, Evander Holyfield meets other successful people—as successful people are often drawn to each other.

"I remember Ted Turner calling me up one time . . . Tiger Woods was playing in a Pro-Am event, playing two holes with everybody," he says. "Turner asked me if I wanted to play a couple of holes with Tiger Woods, and I said, 'no way.' He said, 'Why?' I said, 'Tiger Woods is the best! Why would I want to go out there and play golf with him when I can't beat him?' But then Turner finally admitted that he wanted me to play so that he could go out and play with Woods too. I said, 'Why didn't you just tell me that in the first place?' So I agreed, and Tiger said that he wanted to golf with me first.

"Boxing is a mind thing, like golf. I'm the best because I practice and do things other people ain't willing to do. Let me tell you a story about Cancun.

Down in Cancun, all of the fighters were trying to get me to drink more. Now, I just had one or two, but they were all like, 'Man, Holyfield, I bet I can do more shots than you!' See, I'm not all about that. I do what I love. I don't know why other fighters do it. I don't know if they do it because 'I'm mean' or 'I'm mad' or 'I have to get people back, somebody stole my bike,' or whatever."

It is that level of self-control that allowed Holyfield to be pragmatic about his Olympic disqualification, in which he was DQ'd for hitting his opponent on the break (and knocking out New Zealand's Kevin Barry) in the 1984 games and had to settle for the bronze medal.

"It's a part of life," he says. "I wasn't going to jump up and down and cry about it."

Holyfield went on to turn professional at Madison Square Garden in November of 1985, against the rugged Lionel Byarm—not a typical pro debut opponent, bringing a 9–2–2 record and some measure of main event cachet into the bout. Holyfield won by unanimous decision and in his 11th fight decisioned Dwight Muhammad Qawi in Atlanta to win his first cruiserweight world title. After unifying the cruiserweight titles, Holyfield moved up to heavyweight in 1988 and beat James "Buster" Douglas in 1990 to become the undisputed heavyweight champion of the world. He defended his title against notables, including Larry Holmes and George Foreman, before losing to Riddick Bowe on November 13, 1992, in a fight that is remembered as having delivered one of the best rounds (round 10) in heavyweight boxing history.

Bowe rocked Holyfield with an uppercut to begin the round; however, Holyfield rallied to regain control. He would be knocked down in the next round, as Bowe hung on to win a unanimous decision.

On the subject of losses, Holyfield is ever the optimist.

"One of the biggest things I've learned in boxing is that I used to think I had to be undefeated to be successful. To be great. But now I think they weren't so much losses as setbacks. But setbacks pave the way for a comeback. Setbacks just say that there's more for you to have to learn. I look at my career as far as different eras. I won a bronze medal, so I had a successful amateur career. I was the only cruiserweight in history to never lose a title defense, so my cruiserweight era was a success."

In 1993, Holyfield won the title back from Bowe in a fight that is remembered as much for a bizarre appearance by parachutist James Miller (aka "The Fan Man") as for its boxing. The man began wafting down toward the ring during round 7, when Holyfield implored Bowe to look to the skies. They both looked up and saw the flyer come crashing down near the side of the ring, where he was promptly beaten by members of Bowe's entourage. Perhaps the only thing more dangerous than a champion boxer is his entourage. Holyfield would regain his title that night, and after beating Tyson would join Muhammad Ali as the only fighter to ever win the world title three times.

I ask him if he ever, in his wildest dreams, imagined that he would have the kind of wealth and success that we were surrounded by in that moment. That his children would lay their heads on pillows in a mansion, after the way that he grew up.

"I never had wild dreams," he answers. "I wanted to have a nice family. I thank God because my job allowed me to help all of my brothers and sisters. We came up in tough times, and everybody makes bad decisions, but we don't have a family member that's in the ghetto no more. My happiness comes from the things I'm able to do for others . . . not so much what somebody does for me . . . like the foundation [the Evander Holyfield Foundation], funding the same amateur boxing program [Georgia Amateur Boxing Association] I grew up in, and things like that. That's just a good old feeling within my heart. This is what I do. This is what I like doing."

At one time, Holyfield was beyond outspoken about his born-again Christianity, using every televised appearance as a chance to mention it. In 1994 he was diagnosed with a heart condition, but claimed, after watching televangelist Benny Hinn on television, to be healed of the malady. He would become a frequent guest on Hinn's program. I make several attempts to ask about the state of his faith today.

"Let me tell you a story," he says. "I was in Egypt about three weeks ago, and we toured the Pyramids where the Pharaohs were buried. These Pharaohs, they got gold and they got everything. I see all of the artifacts and everything that showed how great these people are. Now these Pharaohs wanted to be buried with their chariots, because they thought that eventually they were going to come back to life and be able to have all of the riches and things they had before they died. So I'm standing there and the tour guide says, 'Evander, you don't look very impressed.' I just know how they did it. The guide said, 'Will you share it with us?" I said people back then lived to be 600 or 700 years old. I said, you mean to tell me that if people still had the life expectancy they had back then, that you couldn't put up a pyramid? I said think about how foolish these Pharaohs are. Imagine if he comes back with these gold chariots now. What's he going to do with that? They use electricity now. Wherever they go, he's going to be the last one who gets there now! Imagine if you lived 400 years? You would have a lot of doggone kids in 400 years."

I ruminate on that for a moment as Holyfield continues explaining his fascination with the Nile River and how the Egyptians had to transport the raw materials from the Pyramids all the way over from the Nile. It is dark outside Evander Holyfield's pyramid now. I begin to feel a little guilty that Holyfield has returned from Cancun and has barely greeted his kids, spending the majority of the evening with me. I ask him what it's like, today, to be Evander Holyfield.

"People come up to me and say, 'It must be hard to be you,' he says. "But I say, 'Hey it's not hard at all. You don't know how hard it is for people to say nothing to you and just grab their belongings, and hold their purse, because they think you gonna snatch it.' But now people see me and they don't grab their belongings, they smile. They say, 'You made my day.' I like that. I have people say, 'You know what?

You're a good guy.' Evander Holyfield is a good guy, people love him.

"What's hard," he continues, "was being a black kid fighting on an amateur card in the South, knowing you had to knock the other kid out to win, or else you weren't going to get the decision."

He pauses, and I know what's coming.

"But," he says, "it's not like I cried about it."

CHAPTER TWELVE

STEVE LOTT

He who fights with monsters might take care lest
he thereby become a monster. And if you gaze for
long into an abyss, the abyss gazes also into you.

—FRIEDRICH NIETZSCHE

STEVE LOTT IS THROWING punches at my head. I
have agreed to meet one of Mike Tyson's former
managers at his office on 40th Street and 5th Avenue
in Manhattan. It is a space that, apparently, once belonged to William Randolph Hearst. Now it is filled,
from floor to ceiling, with boxing memorabilia and
the aforementioned Lott—proprietor of Hall of Boxing Champions, Inc. One enters through an ornate
doorway on street level and takes a small elevator up
to Lott's suite, where a giant poster of Muhammad
Ali greets visitors as they step out of the elevator.

"Have you been mugged yet?" Lott asks me, as I
enter the space. I immediately make a mental check
of my attire—black T-shirt, fitted jeans, the kind of
bowling-shoes-casual footwear that are in vogue right

now. Black hat. I have tried to look as New Yorkish (read: worn enough black) so as to blend in. However, Lott immediately reads me as a Midwesterner.

Lott has me out of my chair and is showing me the physics behind the slips and weaves that made Mike Tyson special.

"It wasn't just the punching power that made Mike special, it was knowing that he wasn't going to get hit," says Lott. "When Mike walked into the ring and had the confidence that people couldn't touch him, he was unbeatable."

Lott himself is a young-looking man in his early fifties. He has the look of a man who is doing what he wants to do with his hours and minutes. It is a rare look in America. Lott was fortunate to make the acquaintance of Jim Jacobs near the beginning of Tyson's career. Both men were handball players (Lott, the world four-wall handball champ in 1975) and forged a friendship over handball and fight films. Now, along with Brian Cayton (son of Tyson manager Bill), he controls funding from the sale of the world's largest fight film collection and spends his hours acquiring boxing memorabilia from dealers around the world.

"I really like the Hollywood stuff," he says, while showing me hundreds of Polaroids of the boxing posters and films he has acquired. "I'm every collector's sucker, meaning that I'm the first guy they call when they get a new piece. They know I'll buy because I don't want anyone else to get this stuff."

In the corner of the room are boxes filled with fight-worn trunks and gloves. The place is a fight fan's dream. Next to Lott's desk sits a stack of mounted posters, magazine covers, and press photos of Mike Tyson.

"Look at his eyes in these pictures—there's a glimmer about them. His eyes are absolutely dead now." He thumbs through the photos, stopping on a fashion magazine cover featuring Tyson and Joan Jett. "The editors gave Jett the option of doing the cover with any male celebrity—they wanted a man and a woman on the cover," he explains. "She said she wouldn't do it with anybody except Mike Tyson."

I ask Lott about his new endeavor, the Boxing Hall of Champions.

"We're working with a few cities and potential investors on the Boxing Hall of Champions project. It's going to be an interactive experience for fight fans, where they can view films, stand in authentic rings, and really experience boxing."

Lott hands me a pamphlet for the museum project, which looks elaborate and expensive. Over his left shoulder is an oil painting of Tyson throwing the patented left hook, accompanied on the canvas by a rendering of an atomic-bomb mushroom cloud. Over his right shoulder is a painting of Tyson training under the eye of Cus D'Amato.

"Cus taught the techniques to Jose Torres, Floyd Patterson, and Mike. Explosive fighters earn big dollars. And in boxing you're not measured by anything except the amount of money you command. Belts and everything else is secondary. Very early on in their relationship, Cus asked Mike if he wanted to make big money, or if he wanted to make extraordinary money.

Mike, of course, said that he wanted to make extraordinary money. He made Mike perhaps the most sensational fighter to ever walk into a boxing ring."

I ask Lott how he became involved in the fight game, and in Tyson's career.

"Jim and I were handball partners, and he began to bring me in on the management of Mike's career. Mike always said that my job was to make him look good."

How so?

"There was one instance where he was going on one of the morning talk shows with Bryant Gumbel. And Mike was great on these shows. He was so soft spoken that they usually had to turn up his microphones just to hear him. He had on a nice sweater and a gold chain. I pulled him over before he went on and said, 'Gimmie the chain.' After the show he asked me why I made him take off the chain and I told him about the image we were trying to project. He said, 'Just make me look good.'

"Mike was and still is very aware of everything that anyone says or writes about him. He reads everything. His knowledge of the sport and of what's happening in the sport is encyclopedic. When things were going well, from 1985 through 1988, he would go to his room at night, to reflect, and he was happy about what was being said. I can only imagine how he feels now. He was voted the most hated athlete in New York just a few weeks ago. People think that boxers don't reflect or don't have feelings . . . they think fighters are just animals that love violence, but that couldn't be further from the truth. What hurts Mike is knowing that he's no longer loved and adored. Fighters in general need a lot of positive emotional support."

Lott, it seems, provided much of that emotional support for Tyson in the mid-80s as the fighter ascended the heavyweight ranks and through his championship run. Tyson was a frequent visitor to Lott's NYC apartment between fights, as well as the fighter's foray into the New York nightlife scene—exploring his newfound fame and freedom.

Lott also had a great deal of influence on the fighter when it came to the post-fight interview—an in-the-ring affair in which the fighter traditionally spins out cliches about the quality of his opponent and what an honor it was to be in the ring with him. However cliche, it was critical for the Tyson camp to harness the raw fury that made Tyson special those moments before the public-friendly sound bites that would make him marketable outside the ring.

"I remember an incident after the Larry Holmes fight. Mike didn't particularly care for Holmes, and he also didn't like Larry Merchant, who was doing the post-fight interview. I went up to Mike in the ring after the fight and told him exactly what to say. I told Mike to say that he was a great champion and that he regretted having to fight him. To which Mike said, 'Fuck you.' I was worried that he was going to go on the air and blow everything.

"Then Larry Merchant asked him something to the effect of 'Do you feel like this is a passing of the torch?' And Mike said, 'Larry Holmes is a great champion and I regret having to fight him.' He also added, 'In his prime I wouldn't have had a chance against Larry.'"

LOTT IS UP OUT OF the seat again, showing me exactly how Tyson slipped punches in close range.

"Nobody teaches this stuff anymore. I was at a conference recently and had the chance to talk to Calvin Brock. Have you seen him fight?"

I have. Brock is a decent fighter—not especially big or strong, but he seems to have some ring sense and a good punch.

"I asked Calvin a question," says Lott, continuing. "I said, 'If you had a kid who fought, what's the first and most important thing you would teach him?' To which Brock replied, 'Defense.' I said, 'What do you mean by defense?' He said, 'Movement.' I said, 'What do you mean, movement?' He said, 'How to move around the ring,' and I said, 'Yeah, but what do you mean?' He thought for a few seconds and finally said, 'Head movement.' It took him four questions to get there, and Brock is a smart guy."

I ask Lott why more boxing trainers aren't training fighters in "the method."

"In boxing, trainers don't want fighters walking away and going to other trainers who know more than they do. The trainers are unbelievably stupid in this sport . . .

"With the slipping and weaving motions, Mike was willing to put his chin on the line because of the close proximity he needed to the other fighter. These techniques gave Mike tremendous confidence. Every fighter has fears, but champions rise above those fears."

Lott and I both share stories of sparring experiences in the gym, where well-conditioned fighters lock up in the ring and are exhausted after only a few minutes. What used to happen to opponents now happens to an aging Tyson.

"Opponents reacted to Mike in a variety of different ways. Some fighters, like Jose Ribalta, showed no inhibitions. That was a tremendous fight. Another kid he fought—an accomplished fighter out of Chicago named Alfonso Ratliff—clearly did not want to be there. Larry Holmes came to fight. Michael Spinks came to run. Mike's job was to go in there and open up."

"From 1985 to 1988, people wanted to be Mike Tyson when he walked into the ring . . . with the gladiatorial garb and demeanor. He never failed to entertain in the ring, and outside the ring he was a lovely, soft-spoken kid."

I ask how, and when, things went bad.

"Mike was put on a stage. Many things happened once Mike left Bill Cayton."

Following the Michael Spinks fight in 1988, a rift formed between Tyson and Bill Cayton, and many speculate that the source of that rift was Robin Givens. It is believed that Givens, the star of television's *Head of the Class*, was looking to wrest financial power and influence from the Cayton/Jacobs camp. Eventually, Tyson gravitated to Don King. I ask Lott about Tyson's baptism in Don King's church, an event with both religious as well as corporate symbolism.

"With Don, baptizing meant nothing in terms of religious significance. Everyone present was present for Don King's best interests. Don wanted Mike to think like a part of the Don King group. He went from an atmosphere of elegance and sophistication to an atmosphere of surly lowlifes.

"Don brought Mike out to Cleveland and got him laid 55 times a day. He would say things to Mike like, 'We make a great team.'"

I mention that King's dealings with other fighters were a narrative thread in the book. And the fact that what fighters don't say about King often speaks louder than what they'll actually say.

"You add up all he did to the other guys financially and it pales in comparison to what he did to Mike. I sent him letters almost every day in prison begging him to get his own lawyer and accountant, which he never did."

After the rift with Cayton, Tyson replaced trainer Kevin Rooney with a series of cornermen, none as effective as Rooney—one of the few, and largely regarded as the best, teachers of the D'Amato method. Soon, Tyson was surrounded by childhood friends and King lieutenants, such as Rory Holloway and John Horne, who were ill-equipped to manage the world's largest sports personality.

"Rory Holloway literally couldn't change the battery in a handheld radio. He came to me before the Spinks fight and said, 'Steve, my radio don't work.' I said, 'Have you changed the batteries?' He said, 'Huh?' And this man is in charge of the most valuable sports personality on the planet?

"Mike is the party joke of the century now. Unfortunately, the public will not remember him for being a hero; they'll remember him as a surly, tattoo-faced punk. He needs to get people around him to re-instill in him the memory of what he was. People like Lorraine Jacobs and Jose Torres. People just to hang around with him and talk boxing."

We talk about the redemption process and what it would take for the public to reaccept Mike Tyson. Lott rarely gets a chance to speak with Tyson today; however, he wrote him over 400 letters when the fighter was incarcerated.

"It would be wonderful to see Mike again and give him a big hug," says Lott. "I'd like to see the sparkle in his eyes again."

I ask Lott if he thinks Tyson has lost the taste for his sport and if he, as he has said in recent interviews, hates boxing.

"I don't think he hates boxing, I think he hates himself," Lott replies. We discuss a possible shift to broadcasting for Tyson.

"When he starts talking boxing, he's in his element," says Lott. "He knows more than anybody on the planet. He would be a tremendous color guy . . . and he would be tremendous as a commentator on documentaries on old fighters. Make him an emissary of the sport." Lott pauses, choosing his next words carefully. "But to get into the public eye again . . . he knows people laugh at him. He feels it everywhere he goes, and in the hood he may be okay, but where it counts is in corporate America."

"It's painful for me to see how adored he was and how he's treated now. I have this dream . . . it's a recurring dream where Mike holds a press conference and just apologizes for his behavior. He has several people with him on the podium—people I know would accept his apology and support him, like myself, Lorraine [Jacobs], and Jose [Torres].

"But he would probably rather die than talk to Lorraine right now . . . or me. I got his cell phone number and gave him a call. I wanted to take him to one of Budd Schulberg's plays here in New York . . . Schulberg was a huge fight guy and friend of Cus D'Amato's. I left him a message, and either he didn't get it, or, more likely, he doesn't feel comfortable calling me. Everyone reflects . . . when they put their heads down at night to hit the sack. And I think when Mike lays his head down, he thinks about who he was . . . and a time when he walked down the street and was loved and adored.

"With Bill [Cayton] and Jim [Jacobs], it was like surgeons. They looked at every decision from every conceivable angle, and if given the right information, in those days Mike would always make the right decision.

"I'll give you another example," he says. "Once, right after the Tyrell Biggs fight, someone in the media asked Mike what it felt like to be heavyweight champion, to which he replied, 'It's boring.' Right around the same time I put out a press release that said that Mike Tyson was so good that he'd make people forget Muhammad Ali and Joe Louis.

"Shortly thereafter, I got a phone call from Jim Jacobs, who was livid. He was really upset with me, which rarely happened. He said, 'How could you say that about Muhammad Ali?' And he was pissed off at Mike for saying he was bored with being the youngest, richest heavyweight champion in boxing history. He asked me to get Mike and come to his office immediately. He sat us both down and really chewed Mike out for saying what he said. And then he turned to me and started giving me the business about what I wrote in the press release. As he was yelling at me, I could feel this little tap-tap-tap on my foot. It was Mike tapping me with his foot, and he was smiling, as if to say, 'You're getting yours now.'"

CHAPTER THIRTEEN

LOU **SAVARESE**

*It's interesting that you put me in the league with
those illustrious fighters [Muhammad Ali, Joe
Louis, Jack Johnson], but I've proved since my
career I've surpassed them as far my popularity.
I'm the biggest fighter in the history of the sport.
If you don't believe it, check the cash register.*

—MIKE TYSON ON BOXING

THE FIGHT WAS LITERALLY over before it began, on
a freezing cold, rainy night in Glasgow, at Scotland's
National Stadium, June 24, 2000. The public's reaction to what happened was, I think, generally worse
than what actually occured there, which was, in a
nutshell, Lou Savarese being knocked down by a left
hook to the forehead, getting up, being rattled by another Tyson combination, and then being stopped by
referee John Coyle at :38 of the 1st round. It was
what happened in the seconds immediately following
the stoppage that created problems—that is, Tyson
reaching around Coyle to continue battering a hurt

Savarese, a fighter whom he had nothing against, ostensibly, other than the fact that he happened to be in the ring with him. When Coyle finally regained his composure and truly stopped the fight by wedging himself in between the two fighters, Tyson could be seen apologizing to Coyle for his indescretion. Both corners entered the ring and, by raising Tyson's hand, Coyle signaled the end of the fight. There wasn't the usual ring pandemonium or outrage to be seen—that would come later. Tyson would be fined $187,500 for his actions in the bout, but would escape the indignity of losing his right to fight again in Great Britain.

Scottish National Party leader Alex Salmond led the charge, describing the bout as "a farce" and a "complete mis-match" in a BBC interview. He would go on to suggest that those who had supported Tyson should "hang their heads in shame" and that "the so-called economic benefits, on which Jack Straw based his disgraceful decision to let convicted rapist Tyson into Scotland, proved to be totally illusory. Women's groups and the Scottish parliament were absolutely right to oppose this so-called fight. It would have been far better all round if it had never taken place."

Ex-world featherweight champion Barry McGuigan said Tyson should have been disqualified.

"What he did was appalling. He showed complete contempt for authority."

Referring to Tyson's comments, McGuigan said, "Tyson is clearly out of control out of the ring—and out of control in it."

Tyson's lack of control out of it was generating a good deal of press in the United States. On February

8, 2000, Tyson reached settlement with two women whom he allegedly assaulted at a Washington restaurant. They accused Tyson of grabbing one woman and requesting a sexual relationship and swearing at the other woman. The women asked for a total of $7.5 million in damages. Lawyers for both sides agreed to keep terms of the settlement confidential. In May of the same year, Tyson was accused by a topless dancer in a Las Vegas nightclub of punching her in the chest and hurling expletives at her. Police were called to the scene, but after interviewing witnesses, including Tyson himself, they decided not to press charges.

While his nights out were a study in futility, by this time there was no such thing as a Tyson fight without incident, as he seemed incapable of simply riding into town, scoring a quick knockout or stoppage, and riding out, as was earlier the case. Tyson was almost three years to the day removed from the infamous ear-biting Holyfield bout and was coming off a dirty fight with Francois Botha and a no-contest with Orlin Norris in 1999, followed by a laugher with Brit Julius Francis in January of 2000.

"I'm on the Zoloft to keep me from killing y'all," said Tyson in September of the same year. "It has really messed me up, and I don't want to be taking it, but they are concerned about the fact that I am a violent person, almost an animal. And they only want me to be an animal in the ring."

He joins the throngs of American secretaries, salesmen, and housewives taking Zoloft, but, for a celebrity, it becomes national news. I ask Savarese his initial impressions of the fighter upon meeting.

"I didn't really have much interaction with Tyson before the fight," says Savarese, now a successful New York realtor, between appointments. "I first met him at a press conference in London and just remember that he had all of these people around him at all times . . . probably 30 or so people. We were supposed to fight on three or four different occasions, but the fights got canned for this reason or that . . . it kind of sucked when we finally fought because my wife and I wanted it to be a little while after we had had our first son. It's always hard to travel and be away from family, especially after you've just had a kid."

Savarese speaks often of his family—wife Louisa and his two boys Luca and Ciro, ages four and five. He is the son of a cab driver and met Louisa, then a student at the University of Houston, through a mutual friend. She is the daughter of a Harvard grad, and a schoolteacher by trade. He spells her name for me—"just like mine, with an 'a' at the end."

"Louisa must have had an eye problem when she met me," he says. "I'm blessed with a beautiful wife and beautiful kids—too blessed to be depressed. She's not much of a fight fan though . . . and had a hard time watching me fight. Actually, I grew up watching boxing, and my dad was a big fan, but he never wanted us to box. I had a scholarship waiting for me at a university in Florda, if I could have just brought up my grade point average," Savarese remembers. "But that's not something I could do at the time. My wife is the ed-u-ma-cated one in the family, I guess."

Savarese, however, did box, and twice won the New York Golden Gloves title, as well as the Olympic

Sports Festival, before losing in the Olympic trials to
Riddick Bowe. He turned pro in 1989 with a win over
James Smith and notched his first significant victory in
November of 1996, stopping Buster Mathis Jr. in
seven rounds.

I ask Savarese if he had any fear of facing Tyson,
more than the usual pre-fight nerves.

"Not to disrespect him, but I had been in there with
everybody by that point—Foreman, Bowe, all those
guys—and you just get used to fighting. It's your business. My camp went great, and I had a couple of great
sparring sessions right before the fight. To tell you the
truth, if anything I might have been overconfident. I fell
asleep in the dressing room before the fight."

Tyson, of course, was anything but sleepy, jumping on Savarese early with a left hook that hit him
right on the forehead and sent him crashing to the
canvas.

"Tyson was incredibly fast and explosive," he recalls. "When I was young, I used to go up and watch
him fight at the Glens Falls Civic Center in New
York, so I knew he could fight. But he actually covered the distances in the ring faster in real life. There
are two ways to fight Tyson—you can jab and move
around him, or, like Holyfield, you can go right at
him and not back down. I thought I could have continued . . . but as a fighter you always think that. I
think I'd done a pretty good job throughout my career of fighting when I was hurt."

"If it were determined by heart," promoter Lou
DiBella once said of Savarese, "Lou would be undisputed heavyweight champion of the world.'"

Savarese was initially confused about the stoppage when referee Frank Coyle stepped between the two fighters. Initially, he thought that Tyson may have been disqualified for hitting the referee and sending him to the canvas. He has since made his peace with the decision, in the books a TKO 1 for Tyson.

Tyson said in a post-fight interview that he dedicated the win to his best friend, whom he had to bury only weeks prior. When asked how he had trained for the fight, he replied, "I didn't train for this fight, only two or three weeks . . . I dedicated this fight to him. I was gonna rip his heart out. Lennox Lewis, I'm coming for you . . . I'm the most brutal, ruthless champion . . . Lennox Lewis is a conqueror? He's not Alexander, I'm Alexander. I'm Sonny Liston. I'm Jack Dempsey. I'm the best ever . . . my style is impestuous, my defense is impregnable, and I'm just ferocious, I want his heart, I want to eat his children. Praise be to Allah."

His lackeys do what lackeys do best and cheer the schizophrenic interview. Tyson would bow bizarrely to what remained of the Glasgow crowd and then swagger out of the ring surrounded by his group, their jackets emblazoned with the phrase "Be Real."

"Once I said, 'Stop boxing,' the fight was over," said referee John Coyle after the bout. "I gave him every chance . . . but all's well that ends well, and the boy is fine."

Truer words were perhaps never spoken in boxing.

"You know, I'm a big believer in the idea that everything happens for a reason," Savarese says.

"Maybe if I'd continued, Mike would have really hurt me. He was a really devastating puncher."

SINCE HIS RETIREMNT in 2002, Savarese has channeled his considerable work ethic into his real estate business and a burgeoning acting career. What the Tyson fight did for either fighter is debatable—it probably continued Tyson's downward spiral into the bizarre, while it compelled Savarese to continue fighting, much to the dismay of family and friends, who encouraged him to retire after the Tyson bout.

"I've been doing real estate for 10 or 11 years now. I don't know what I'm doing," he says in typical self-deprecating fashion, "but I enjoy it and I just keep buying up these little condos and properties."

Savarese also had a turn as Max Baer in ESPN's docudrama on the life of James Braddock. He equates acting to fighting, in that you often have only one brief opportunity to show what you can do.

"I had an audition for a part recently and I just completely sucked," he says. "I read the lines and I was so terrible . . . the lady reading with me actually asked me if I wanted to do it again. I said, 'Of course.' But in boxing you don't really get the second chances. In a way it's almost the same though—you get a call, you walk in, and you get to perform in front of people. It's extremely nerve-racking.

"I also just wrapped a picture with Burt Young called *Nicky's Game*, about a guy from the Ivy League who sets up this card game in New York. It actually just screened at the New York Independent Film Festival."

Savarese also has credits on *Law and Order: Special Victims Unit* and *The Sopranos* on his acting resume, but it is his boxing legacy that concerns us now.

"Max Kellerman once called me an old-school fighter," says Savarese, when I asked him what he is most proud of in the sport. "He said I had an old-school career."

In addition to a big win over James "Buster" Douglas that advanced Savarese into the national spotlight, he also notched a victory over late-90s contender Lance "Mount" Whitaker, overcoming a 5th round knockdown to win the decision. However, it was steps up in competition that resulted in losses to Michael Grant, Riddick Bowe, and a comebacking George Foreman.

"Foreman did everything right in his comeback," says Savarese. "A lot of older guys bullshit around in there and can win themselves fights . . . it's kind of a catch-22, in that you have a whole lot of ring savvy that you didn't have when you were young. But Foreman did his comeback the right way . . . if you think about who he fought, he always fought guys that were perfect for him . . . guys like me who came forward."

While Savarese lost for the first time at the hands of Foreman, he nevertheless impressed boxing insiders and fans, many of whom felt he deserved the split decision that was given to Foreman. Savarese lost on scorecards of 110–118, 112–115, and a favorable 114–113.

Our conversation wanders a bit as we discuss who I have interviewed for this project ("Tyrell Biggs is a great guy . . . Mitch Green is crazy!") and Savarese's favorite fighters from bygone eras ("I loved

Marvin Hagler, he used to run 15 miles a day . . . and he got out and stayed out.") I know that Savarese has a closing to get to, so I do my best to try to wrap the interview. He is, however, clearly enjoying talking about the names and personalities from his sport. I ask Savarese if he misses the actual boxing.

"Only about 23 hours a day," he says. "I miss the training. I was one of those guys that just loved going to the gym. They talk about guys who were all talent but no heart, and I was pretty much the opposite. I miss the cameraderie. There are a lot of characters in boxing, but 99 percent of the people in this sport are good people. There's not much false bravado.

"It's tempting right now for guys like me, because the division seems so wide open. I see a bunch of guys from my era making comebacks. I heard that Tim Witherspoon fought recently . . . and I know that Mitch Green fought a guy down in Memphis. I really think Tyson and Riddick Bowe could have gone down in history as two of the greatest heavyweights in history," Savarese continues. "Not to be cliche, but Mike Tyson had great fundamentals early in his career. He was moving his head and he fought in clinches, which is what he stopped doing later on. In the early days, if you found yourself in a clinch with Tyson, you were in trouble."

Savarese was scheduled to fight again, in October of 2005 against the 40-year-old Ronald Bellamy, in a bout to raise money for the family of former Chester resident Lou Allen, with the all of his purse going to First Lieutenant Allen's widow and four children. He ruptured a bicep in training, however, and to date, the fight has not been rescheduled. From the tone of our conversation, Savarese considers himself retired, although he is still an avid viewer of old fight films and has become something of a student of George Foreman's comeback. His humility keeps him from comparing himself to any particular old-school boxer, although he admires Joe Louis for his ability to both box and punch. A glance at his ring record indicates that Savarese has fought many of the best the division has had to offer across eras—spanning George Foreman to Kirk Johnson. The boxing records archive (Boxrec.com) is a vast resource linking every professional boxer, current and former, with all opponents. Even the casual boxing fan can lose himself for hours. Everything is there on the screen—looking very neat and orderly, quite unlike the sport itself, which is anything but. These records are smooth and convenient because they fail to mention anything about drug problems or people getting ripped off—two topics germane to the ring life. The long, winding genealogies are almost biblical in nature.

His record stands at 43 wins and 6 losses, with 35 wins by knockout. I ask Savarese, finally, what he would say to Tyson, also an old New Yorker, if they ever crossed paths again.

"Actually, it's funny you mention that," he says. "I was down in Fort Lauderdale at one of the casinos there . . . the Hard Rock . . . for a fight show not too long ago. And believe it or not, I literally bumped into Mike Tyson in a hallway. Now back in the old days, Mike was always surrounded by 30 or 40 guys, none of whom, excuse my French, really ever gave a shit about him. It was absurd the way they acted back then . . . jumping up and down and hollering. But anyway, when I bumped into him in Florida, he remembered me and gave me a big hug. I asked him how he was doing. 'Not too good,' he said. 'I've got a lot of problems . . . I'm about 50–50.' So we said our good-byes and kept on walking. Mike is kind of an enigma. Sometimes you feel sorry for him . . . sometimes you feel afraid of him or what he's going to do.

"After a few steps my friend and I looked back, and there was Tyson, just standing there with his hands in his pockets. All by himself."

THE ANDREW GOLOTA **INTERLUDE**

I AM WAITING ON THE telephone to get the phone number for a grown man named Ziggy. Andrew Golota's trainer, Sam Colonna, is looking around for the number. I hear gym noises in the background—the thwack thwack of the speed bag, and the little electronic bell that anyone who has spent any time around boxing gyms recognizes. The black kid who answered the phone wasn't going to get Colonna for me (said he was busy), until I told him I was writing a book about Tyson, and that I needed him for an interview.

After a clipped conversation with Colonna, and an even more clipped conversation with Golota himself, I finally phone Ziggy, who is on a car phone. The conversation goes something like this:

Me: I talked to Andrew and it looks like he's not interested . . . but his story is really compelling and I'd hate to write a Tyson book without him. Is there anything you can do? (When I talked to Golota, he sounded pretty depressed. At the time of the call, he was just a few weeks removed from a one-round knockout loss at the hands of the not-so-legendary Lamon Brewster.)

Ziggy: What do you want me to do? You want me to kick his ass? (Ziggy belly laughs. At this point I should also add that he has a not thick, but still discernable, Eastern European accent. I imagine a big, middle-aged guy wearing a blue Adidas warmup suit. I hope that when we meet he actually looks like this.)

Me: What?

Ziggy: I'm bigger and tougher than that bastard. (Awkward silence here before I chuckle the chuckle of someone who doesn't quite know how to take what he's just heard. Ziggy senses this and starts talking again.) You know what your problem was?

Me: What?

Ziggy: You mentioned Tyson! He probably pissed down his leg! (I laugh uncomfortably, remembering how sad Andrew sounded on the phone. I felt the discomfort that one feels for the big, dumb bully in the movies—the one who doesn't know he's being made fun of. This is not to say that Golota is dumb in any way. Ziggy and I agree to talk again in a few days.)

The fight itself was a study in all things bizarre. For starters, it was in a bizarre location, Detroit, Michigan. Actually, Auburn Hills, which is about 40 minutes north of town, up I–75. The real Detroiters having no reason to come up here besides the Pistons and several outlet malls. It is the picture of suburbia. A strange place for Mike Tyson to go to work. The

arena is filled with a strange mix of Detroit auto in-
dustry money, Detroit ghetto, and Southeast Michigan tough-guy. It's a pretty combustible mix of
people. The problem with big fights in big cities not
used to hosting boxing is that their fight fans often
don't know what to do with themselves. The spectre
of live violence is often a little bit too much for them.
This will come into play later.

Tyson's ring walk is typically sinister. This time he
wears a white towel, torn at the center, which hangs
off his shoulder. He paces the ring like a caged animal, in the usual Tyson way. Frank Garza, the referee, is trying to get the entourages out of the ring.
Incidentally, Tyson's entourage got bigger and his career got worse. By this time, there are men in tuxe-
dos, bandannas, ball caps, and everything in between
milling self-importantly around Tyson. There is a
man with the word "shit" emblazoned in rhinestones
on his hat. It is their moment in the sun and they are
not about to listen to Garza.

Finally, it is just Tyson and Golota in the ring, and
the much larger man, Golota, looks extremely stiff.
His long legs seem permanently locked at the knees.
He pushes a jab occasionally in the direction of Tyson,
sometimes following it with an awkward-looking left-
hook that resembles a man stirring a big pot of soup.
It is wholly ineffective. Tyson, however, is less efficient
than usual. He is clearly hunting for the bomb, the
knockout punch, and although he came in at a re-
spectable 222 pounds, his movements are slower and
fewer than before. His combinations are few, but he
catches Golota with a huge right hand on the tip of

his chin, and the big man falls backward onto the seat of his trunks. Tyson walks to the neutral corner. Rather, the momentum of the punch just naturally carries him there. He glances over his shoulder momentarily to sneer at Golota, as if to tell him to stay on the canvas if he knows what's good for him.

After figuring out that he could land the overhand right at will, Tyson begins doing so, hurting Golota on several occasions and opening cuts on the big Pole's face. While Golota seemed frustrated and was largely throwing slapping arm punches at Tyson, he should be given credit for standing and throwing toe to toe with him in the 2nd round. However, near the end of the one-minute break between rounds, Golota informed his corner that he was done, despite the fact that they were trying to shove his mouthpiece into his mouth and force him out for round 3. Garza gave Golota one last chance, informing him that the bell would ring in a few seconds and it would be all over. Golota, looking angry, shoved Garza and shoved at his handlers, who were by now pleading with him to avoid the embarassment of quitting and go out on his shield. Tyson, for his part, had to be restrained by his entourage. He wanted more violence, and a mere TKO would not satisfy him tonight in the city that gave us Motown, race riots, and, of late, lots of violence. On his way out of the ring, Golota was pelted by beer, pop, and garbage.

I AM IN ZIGGY ROSALSKI'S Auto Body Shop in Jersey City, New Jersey. He owns several properties in this area, I learn, as well as the boxing gym across the street—a project started by Rocky Marciano's brother in the 1970's and finished by Ziggy Rosalski.

"I came over from Poland 30 years ago without a penny to my name . . . I would do any work—shovel shit—anything to be working," he says.

Rosalski is a large man, about six foot three, with a crew cut and barrel chest. He rolls up to our meeting in a giant banana-yellow Humvee. Clearly, he is a man of some means. The body shop is exactly how you would envision a New Jersey body shop—there is hot pink involved in the interior, along with black marble countertops. It is tackily swank. I ask him how he came to know Andrew Golota.

"He came to my gym in 1995 and we became friends. I helped him through some legal troubles with the Polish government. You know, just helped him with the paperwork."

The gym itself is impeccable—an aberration in the boxing world. Rosalski sees to it that the place is perpetually clean—one could eat off the workout equipment and the ring canvas. There are a handful of people working out on the various weight machines and a young black guy in the ring, shuffling and working on technique.

Andrew Golota was born January 5, 1968, in Warsaw, Poland, and, it is written, originally immigrated to Chicago after winning a bronze medal in the 1988 Olympics, to look for work as a truck driver. He was directed to a gym and turned pro in 1992. He fought often in the early years, racking up eight wins in 1992 and seven in 1993, running his record to 28–0 before two bizarre losses to Riddick Bowe, back to back, in 1996. He was next knocked out in a round by Lennox Lewis in October of 1997. To say that Golota at times had self-control issues would be to vastly understate things. Golota, affectionately nick-named "The Foul Pole," is known for bizarre behavior—headbutts, low blows, disqualifications.

The Bowe fights were his most noteworthy—perhaps the high points of his career—and several title shots were all brokered by Don King.

"Don King got us three title shots, against Chris Byrd [a draw, which many thought Golota should have won], Johnny Ruiz [L UD 12], and Lamon Brewster [L TKO 1]. Everybody talks bad about Don, but he is the only guy that would give us a chance after the Tyson fight, the only guy who would return my calls.

"Training for the Tyson fight went very well. Andrew was a great fighter in the gym. He has amazing skills and physical ability. His downfall is fear and his nerves.

"He fractured his cheekbone in sparring three weeks before the fight and didn't want to go through with it. But his trainer at the time, Al Certo, was an old-school guy. Certo called him a baby, told him he should take the fight.

"He told me he was dizzy in there and that he didn't want to keep fighting. Me, Certo, and Danny Milano were working his corner that night—we tried to get him to go out and keep fighting. We were practically shoving the mouthpiece in his mouth and pushing him out there because he wasn't doing too bad, really."

When the Golota camp went to the hospital to get cuts stitched up, an X-ray confirmed that the fractured cheekbone had actually worsened as a result of the fight.

FRANK GARZA REFEREED the Tyson/Golota bout, and I ran into him recently at a benefit show to keep Detroit's famed Kronk Gym alive. We are surrounded by moneyed Detroiters dressed to the teeth—the best society has to offer—cheering for blood as two young pros hammer each other for their enjoyment in the first four-rounder of the night. Garza is a small man, probably around five feet nine inches and 150 pounds. I ask him what it was like to be charged with keeping tabs on two of the most powerful, and unpredictable, forces in the heavyweight division.

"I didn't ask for the fight," he says. "I was sitting at home and I got a phone call from the commission, letting me know I was working the fight. I treated it like any other fight. I wasn't nervous at all, because at the end of the day I have my company and I have my wife. I'm content. But that said, I still ran through over 100 scenarios in my mind of things that could happen during the fight. But I never dreamed that one of the fighters would quit in his corner after the second round."

Perhaps Garza's biggest challenge was clearing the army of lackeys and hangers-on out of the ring so that he could give his pre-fight instructions. I ask his impressions of Tyson the person, based on their interactions.

"Mike Tyson was probably the most honest person I've ever met. He says whatever is on his mind . . . and he's perfect for boxing, because in boxing, in that ring, you can say and do and think whatever you want. It is the most American place in America. It is truly politically correct."

THE POLISH MEDIA brutalized Andrew Golota for the better part of three years after the Tyson fight. Golota is inactive, but contacted Rosalski recently, saying he was interested in pursuing another title shot.

"Andrew doesn't need boxing—his wife is an attorney, and he has made a great deal of money in the ring," says Rosalski. "But I truly think he loves the sport. He loves the training and is in great condition.

"Like I said before, I called ESPN, Showtime, and HBO, and they all slammed the door in our faces. Don [King] was the only guy that would return my calls. He loves Andrew—says we have the Polish Tyson. He recognizes that the fans love him as well. His last fight in Chicago drew almost 20,000 people. Don King is a great promoter. Don treated us like family."

Golota, still looking for a title, has contacted Rosalki about setting up additional fights. Rosalski is trying to match his fighter carefully.

"Honestly, I want to put him in there with another old guy," he says. "I'd like to get a fight with Evander Holyfield. Evander is old, Andrew is old. They can't hurt each other. Andrew is 37 and he's my friend—we go fishing and skiiing together. I don't want to see him get hurt."

We discuss other names—Mitch Green, Tony Tubbs—80s-vintage heavyweights with names who would provide an easy mark for the aging Golota. Finally, I ask Rosalski what drew him to the sport of boxing.

"I don't really like it much, honestly. I worry. Whenever I'm working a corner, I pray before every fight—I pray for my guy and I also pray for the opponent. I get sick to my stomach. We saw a guy die on an undercard of one of our fights. He got knocked out and went into a coma. Died three days later. I didn't sleep for three weeks."

CHAPTER FOURTEEN

LENNOX **LEWIS**

Let your plans be dark and impenetrable as night,
and when you move, fall like a thunderbolt.

—SUN TZU, *THE ART OF WAR*

THIS WAS PERHAPS Mike Tyson's most troubled period—the period where all of the problems came to a
head and became tragically public. Tyson, clad in
black and looking sinister, grabs his crotch and
screams epithets at the media at a pre-fight press conference. He says, "I wish that you guys had children
so that I could kick them in the fucking head or
stomp on their testicles so that you could feel my
pain, because that's the pain I wake up to every day."
The same press conference would later erupt into an
all-out brawl, with Tyson later admitting that he bit
Lennox Lewis on the leg during the fracas. He tells a
female journalist, "I normally don't do interviews
with women unless I fornicate with them . . . so you
shouldn't talk anymore unless you want to, you
know." He tells Lennox Lewis, now famously, that he

wishes to eat his children. He is escorted out of a Havana hotel after throwing glass Christmas ornaments at a group of journalists wishing to interview him. No charges were pressed.

Yet, there is a child-likeness about Mike Tyson . . . namely his proclivity for saying whatever is on his mind at the moment it ends up there. The feeling that he never wanted to be the black man who made you want to walk to the other side of the street. And while he is getting his ass handed to him by Lennox Lewis, you end up feeling for him. Feeling sorry. You see him backstage with his kids—both eyes cut and badly disfigured. He says that he will fade into "bolivian" and you hope that he does, and you hope, even just a little, that "bolivian" is kind to him.

"I feel like sometimes that I was born, that I'm not meant for this society because everyone here is a fucking hypocrite," said Tyson in a pre-fight interview with ESPN.com. "Everybody says they believe in God, but they don't do God's work. Everybody counteracts what God is really about. If Jesus was here, do you think he would show me any love? Do you think Jesus would love me? I'm a Muslim but . . . I think Jesus would have a drink with me and discuss . . . why you acting like that? Now I think he would be cool. He would talk to me. No Christian ever did that and said in the name of Jesus even . . . They'd throw me in jail and write bad articles about me and then go to church on Sunday and say that Jesus is a wonderful man and he's coming back to save us. But they don't understand that when he comes back, these crazy greedy capitalistic men are gonna kill him again."

TODAY LENNOX LEWIS is enjoying that rarest of occupations—the privilege of largely being paid just to travel around and be Lennox Lewis. Tonight we are both at a swank fundraiser for the famed Kronk Gym in Detroit. The city is trying to close the gym (producer of world champion Thomas Hearns, among others) and boxing's royalty has come out to show its support. The room, in the city's historic Fisher Building, is gilded—lots of velvet, gold, and Rennaisance era architecture. In the center of the room is a boxing ring, which I always think looks out of place in rooms like this—like the guy who didn't get the memo about black tie and ends up showing up in jeans and a golf shirt.

Entrance is everything at these events, and Lewis shows up fashionably late, surrounded by the requisite throng of personal assistants (oddly, another tall guy in dreadlocks who looks just like Lewis) and PR reps. Lewis is one of the rare athletes who looks as big, or bigger, in real life than his numbers would indicate. He is tall and carries himself with the necessary celebrity swagger. He could be an NFL defensive end, on looks alone. I've noticed that entering a building with a throng always draws more of a throng. Soon Lewis is surrounded by autograph seekers, women of indiscriminate age in low-cut cocktail dresses, and cameras. I overhear several women in the hors'd'oeuvres line indicate that they will be marrying Lennox Lewis, as he is the rare fighter—chalk it up to a British accent, the dreadlocks, or whatever—who seems to project an image of sophistication and class. Security people, both uniformed and otherwise, make motions with their arms indicating to the crowd that they will need to make way for Lewis. The crowd makes way, but just a little bit. This is all very important. Aretha Franklin (long, white fur coat—she looked great) just made this trek with her own impressive throng a few moments ago.

The little pack meanders its way through the crowded lobby and into the ring area, where Lewis is seated at ringside. He embraces his trainer for the Tyson fight, Emmanuel Steward, and the two pose for photographers. The throng is ushered away, and Lewis sits quietly at ringside watching two club fighters pound out a prelim fight, surrounded by all of the food, drink, adulation, and beauty the human heart could imagine. He looks supremely bored.

BEFORE THE MIKE TYSON fight, it could be said that Lewis's legacy needed a little bit of work. Like Tyrell Biggs, he was an Olympian (gold, super heavyweight, 1998) of Olympian physical proportions, with the tools to bang and thus become a Boxing Hero. Rather, he fought cautiously, winning fights but never winning the all important fascination of the public. He lost, surprisingly by knockout, to Hasim Rachman and by TKO to Oliver McCall—both fighters considered to be inferior to Lewis. He was a little too self-controlled for this public, who were waddling fat and satisfied out of the buffet of violence that Mike Tyson had served them for so many years.

"You know when you go into a barbershop to get your hair cut?" asks Lewis. "You go in there and you hear rumors . . . you hear whispers about how if I never fought Tyson there would always be questions."

Lewis, newly married as of a few months ago, is telling me this on the telephone while attempting to order lunch for his children in a noisy restaurant. Turkey and water . . . hold the cilantro. Children's voices can be heard chattering away in the background. I ask him about preparations and motivations for the fight, in light of Tyson's bombastic pre-fight behavior.

"The preparation was easy, because he attacked me at a press conference and it really kind of got under my skin," says Lewis with a British matter-of-factness of the press conference in which Tyson allegedly bit his leg. "I was like, 'Why is this guy biting me?' The fact of the matter is that I'm just not one of those guys. He really antagonized me. I said, 'Why is he carrying on like this?' Me, I'm one of those 'search and destroy,' laid back types, I guess . . . the kind of guy that if the lights go off in a room and everybody is on the floor going crazy, I'll be the guy just sitting in the corner sorting it out."

It is that kind of systematic sorting that allowed Lewis to realize that he didn't want to be a boxer his entire life. He also harbors no fantasies of beating a prime Muhammad Ali, as evidenced by his post on a BBC fan forum.

"If I could fight anyone, it would be Jack Johnson—he was so ahead of his time," said Lewis. "I would like to have the opportunity to fight Tyson too, and I'm sure it will arise if he can face me. I would not like to have fought Muhammad Ali, as I have too much respect for him on a personal and professional level. Larry Holmes, Ali's ex-sparring partner, fought

Muhammad Ali and hated himself after giving him an unnecessary beating after winning. The only reason he won was because of Ali's aging boxing skills."

Lewis is currently doing guest boxing commentating and reading film scripts, splitting his time between New York City, Miami, and Jamaica. Lewis, born in London in 1965, the son of a mechanic and a nursing home worker, was raised with "proper values" that he says were instilled by his mother.

"I came from East London, and we rolled by a different ball there," he says. "We were raised to have honor among friends and to honor our mothers. Mother didn't really like the boxing at first," he recalls. "But it was a thing that kept me occupied and kept me out of trouble. I enjoyed the challenge and the individuality . . . the fact that you didn't have to rely on a team and that it all depends on you. It comes down to strategy, speed, and quickness."

Lewis used that speed and quickness to represent Canada in the 1984 Olympic games, eventually losing in the quarterfinals to Tyrell Biggs. He would win gold in the 1988 Olympics in Seoul, Korea, as a super heavyweight, again fighting under the Canadian flag. He stopped American Riddick Bowe in the 2nd round to win gold, and it would be Bowe who would refuse to fight him several years later, giving Lewis his first world title. Lewis turned pro in 1989 and notched several wins in Canada and England, before beating notable (albeit, by that time older) American heavyweights Mike Weaver (TKO 6) and Tyrell Biggs (TKO 3) in 1991. He collected the European heavyweight title, British heavyweight title, and Commonwealth heavyweight title before being awarded the WBC heavyweight title in 1993 when Riddick Bowe refused to fight him. He would lose the belt on a 2nd-round TKO to Oliver McCall in 1994, but would win it back in 1997, eventually unifying the titles by defeating Evander Holyfield in 1999. A loss to Hasim Rachman in 2001 (which was avenged in his next fight) is the only other blemish on Lewis's impressive resume.

"Losing . . . it kind of puts everything in perspective," he says. "It's humbling. I had a trainer jump ship when I lost . . . because he thought the ship was sinking, but then I realized that the people who left were just cheerleaders and they weren't really helping me."

Lewis, having enlisted legendary trainer Emmanuel Steward, still felt that he needed to defeat Tyson to close the book on his career.

"Yeah, that's the ego aspect of the whole thing," he continues. "I knew Tyson from before though, because we sparred together. I had heard about this young kid who couldn't get anyone to spar with him and I needed sparring, so I went up to the Catskills to meet Tyson and Cus D'Amato. He was a nice guy, came up to me and introduced himself, shook my hand. But then when the bell rang he rushed directly over to my corner and tried to take my head off . . . I did my Muhammad Ali thing at the time and danced around . . . but he helped me learn something up there. He helped me learn that boxing is a hurt business, whereas I was still in the amateur mind-set of moving around and scoring points."

Coming into the fight, Lewis was an 8 to 5 favorite and also enjoyed a 13-inch reach advantage, which in earlier Tyson eras may not have been problematic, but would play a big role in this fight. In the previous 11 years, Tyson had fought only one top heavyweight—Evander Holyfield—and had lost twice. HBO's Larry Merchant even went so far as to say that his reputation was "a sham" and was developed against "inferior competition." He had a point. It could be argued that Tyson had really never fought anyone good and, when he did, he lost.

The bout, on June 8, 2002, at the Pyrmamid in Memphis, was clearly being billed as a morality tale of good versus evil, with the line literally being drawn in the center of the ring by yellow-jacketed security personel pulled straight from a variety of Memphis area Gold's Gyms. It would be refereed by Eddie Cotton—himelf going about six feet five inches and 230—so as to attempt to keep control of the wild personalities (read: Tyson) in the ring.

"I knew for a long time that the fight was mine," Lewis says. "I had spent the last several years among champions and fighting champions, whereas Tyson had been incarcerated and had been having dramas on the road . . . his life was like an open book. I knew he was intimidated by me because I was a lot bigger than he was . . . and because he was acting so skittish and erratic."

Lewis showed no fear as he entered the ring looking fit and ready, while Tyson looked relatively soft and smooth at 234. They each stalked their respective portions of the ring, Lewis was introduced by Jimmy Lennon Jr., while Tyson received a bombastic introduction by boxing legend Michael Buffer. They would fight, he said, for the "linear, legitimate, and universally recognized heavyweight championship of the world."

In the 1st round, Tyson, trained this time by Ronnie Shields, looked frenetic, showing glimpses of the head movement that once made him special. Lewis, on the other hand, looked relaxed, utilizing a long jab and strong clinches that would eventually wear down and frustrate Tyson. In the early rounds Lewis's most effective punches were uppercuts—odd that he was using this punch to hurt the supposed king of the uppercut.

By the end of the 3rd round, Lewis is landing the jab at will and Tyson is cut—his corner a flurry of negative energy. His plan, clearly, hasn't worked, and Shields has been reduced to screaming vague bits of encouragement while the cutman applies pressure and swabs Tyson's nose with astringent. HBO seems obsessed with superclose shots of Tyson's battered face, and it is a sad final look at a once-proud champion. Tyson moans in agony between rounds but, to his credit, comes out at each bell and continues to move forward.

"At that time he was working with people who weren't doing anything for him," says Lewis, of Tyson's corner.

Tyson is down in round 4 as the result of what is ruled a push, but looks suspiciously like a wicked straight right to the middle of Tyson's forehead. Between rounds, Emmanuel Steward encourages his fighter to "just get this motherfucker out of there!" Lewis, however, seems completely relaxed and, perhaps, enjoys prolonging Tyson's beating.

"Emmanuel was the person to sharpen what was dull in me," he says. "He corrected a number of technical problems that I had in the ring. For example, when I fought Ray Mercer, he hit me in the face with his jab pretty much whenever he wanted to, and it's because I was carrying my right hand over on the side of my face to protect against big left-hookers who tried to jump around and attack from the side. I had always carried my hand that way, but Emmanuel encouraged me to bring the hand around to the front of my face. He improved my footwork as well. He got me to believe that I could throw certain combinations."

Does the trainer make the fighter, or does the fighter make the trainer?

"I'm not sure," Lewis says, unwilling to venture into this controversial territory. "All I know is that we helped each other and we were a great team."

At the end of round 7, both of Tyson's eyes are swollen beyond recognition, and he is the picture of utter frustration and honesty in his corner. Shields implores him to throw more punches, to which Tyson replies, barely audible, "I can't."

He is knocked out in the 8th round.

"WHEN I WAS UP in the Catskills sparring, Cus D'Amato said before I left that he was sure that Tyson and I would meet in the ring," says Lewis. "He must have seen something in me, sparring during those day. I know he'd passed, but I wish he could have seen it."

Lewis retired in 2003 with a career record of 41–2–1. Unlike so many of his contemporaries, he retired and stayed retired and plans to pursue his passion for acting, having caught the bug during an appearance in the George Clooney movie *Ocean's 11*.

"Everything I do, I want to do it positively, whether it's as an action hero in a movie or as an entrepreneur," he says. "It's funny, once you have some assets, people start coming at you every day with ideas."

I hear a great deal of commotion in the background during our call; it seems that people are coming up to him constantly with ideas as we speak. He keeps his children from burning their mouths on a fresh sandwich ("Hot, hot, hot!") and answers a variety of questions off-phone. When we reconnect, I ask him if he still communicates with Clooney or any of the other members of the cast, as it was rumored that they may make an appearance at the Detroit Kronk Gym fund-raiser (they didn't).

"Entertainers always know each other," he explains, "so yeah, I could walk into a room and say 'Hey, George, what's happening?' and he would talk to me."

I imagine this scenario for a moment. It's a room into which I would almost certainly not be allowed access. I want to ask Lewis about fame lost, but he continues on, about Tyson.

"A friend of mine saw him down in Miami recently," he says. "Have you seen him recently?"

I remark that I have not seen him since his last fight in June, 2005, in Washington, DC.

"Well, my friend said he wasn't looking too healthy. It's difficult, man. He attracts people that don't do him any good, and he's been used and abused in this business. I hope he can take care of himself, you know, he has kids now, and when you have kids it changes your perspective on everything."

I can hear the sounds of toddlers in the background, and Lewis clearly enjoying their company. I ask him what he might say to Tyson if they have occasion to meet, and he is silent for a moment.

"You know, I don't know," he says finally. "I mean, you can say everything you want to say, but he has to make a decision to change. What I really think he needs," Lewis says finally, "is a proper mother."

CHAPTER FIFTEEN

KEVIN McBRIDE

Only after disaster can we be resurrected.

—TYLER DURDEN, *FIGHT CLUB*

KEVIN MCBRIDE IS FLIRTING shamelessly with our waitress at the Holiday Inn in Boston. She is a woman of indiscriminate age—could be 22 or 40—and is not unattractive. McBride grabs her hand playfully. Asks her if she recognizes his face (she didn't) while smiling up in her direction. A hand is stealthily placed around a waist. A joke is made about how we'll have to increase the tip (by me). McBride finds out that she is from Europe, hasn't been in the states very long. He likes her accent. She probably wonders why America wasn't all she hoped and dreamed, probably reads *People* magazine at night in a small apartment, or perhaps she's working her way through school.

You may ask yourself how it's possible to like someone so unabashedly conceited—but you do. McBride is as good-natured as he is huge. A friendly giant in a Patriots sweatshirt and skullcap. He's the kind of friend you wished you had, the kind of guy who was never in a bad mood and would always provide a good time.

McBride and his trainer/friend Paschal "Packi" Collins have driven through a nasty Nor'easter to make our meeting today. And as the snow fell the previous evening, I spent the greater part of the night traveling the three miles between Boston Logan Airport and the Boston Logan Airport Holiday Inn, crammed into a shuttle bus with what seemed like 80 people, all from the same company and all buzzed on being "snowed in." All I could think about in the bus (besides wanting to get out and walk) was how much I doubted that McBride and Collins would actually show. But they did, on time, and they are clearly having a ball talking about beating Mike Tyson.

"Let me tell you a funny story," says Collins. "I was going into Tyson's dressing room before the fight, watching them wrap his hands, which is a standard procedure where the opposing trainer gets to check the opponent's wraps. I didn't know what the hell was going to face me in there, if they were going to try to intimidate, if they were going to have a big posse going. When I did go in I actually felt quite at ease, because they were very respectful people. They brought in the entourage and all the crew . . . Ali came in . . . which personally I don't agree with. I believe that a fighter should be alone with his thoughts before he fights."

Collins talks with the same thick Irish brogue as McBride and has been with the big fighter since the beginning of his pro career, when the heavyweight was 19. Collins also fights professionally and is a big believer in the psychological edge.

"Our challenge was to get Kevin to believe that he could beat Mike Tyson," he continues. "So when I left Tyson's dressing room, I went back to Kevin and told him that Tyson's hands were shaking so badly that they couldn't even wrap them. It took them like half an hour to wrap them . . . which was pure bullshit. As a result, Kevin was very confident walking into the ring. He was actually relaxed anyway . . . he was fixing his hair on the way to the ring. And then he took the Irish flag in his hands and started waving it when he got in the ring."

I ask McBride why he was so relaxed.

"He trained harder," says Collins. "And Kevin was the bigger man."

"I had this image of him as a fierce and powerful man," says McBride. "I used to watch his fights religiously in Ireland. We'd have to get up at four in the morning to watch them, because of the time difference, but I've wanted to meet him since I was nine years old. It was enough just shaking his hand, much less fighting him. I knew I could beat him," he says, "but the odds were long against me. My mother, who didn't have much money at all, put 200 Euro on me to win, and I actually gave my last $500 to a guy to bet on me. And you know what? I shocked myself!

"I believed I could beat him," says McBride, working on a ham and cheese omelet. "But walking into the ring that night I have to admit I also wondered what the hell I had gotten myself into."

McBRIDE, NICKNAMED "The Clones Colossus," was born in Clones, Ireland, in 1973 and stands 6 feet 6 inches tall, weighing in the neighborhood of 270 pounds. He began boxing at age "10 or 13 . . . or maybe 9," when he used to watch Stevie "The Celtic Warrior" Collins, former WBO super middleweight champion and brother of Packi.

It's been a long time. We all share a laugh.

"Boxing is an adrenaline rush," says McBride. "It's pure adrenaline that I can't really describe. I love the uncertainty of it. I love that you can be behind on the scorecards for nine rounds and then come back and score a 10th-round knockout. It's not over until the fat lady sings."

After an impressive amateur career, in which he was the youngest fighter to win an Irish junior title after only six fights, McBride turned pro at 19 and carved out a 33–4–1 record by fighting often. He would take fights on short notice, sometimes in his opponent's backyard, where decisions are hard to come by.

"We traveled the world," says Collins.

McBride's pro opponents offered little in the way of experience or wins on their resume. His first real test was a 2002 bout in Las Vegas with Davarryl "Touch of Sleep" Williamson, which he lost on a 5th-round stoppage. He was then inactive for all of 2004, before beating Kevin Montiy (15–2–1) on ESPN2.

"Teddy Atlas said I was slow, after I stopped Kevin Montiy on ESPN2," McBride says. "But in a way it was a blessing because in me the Tyson camp thought they had a tailor-made opponent—big, slow, and white. But I'm 270 pounds. I'm not in there to look pretty or win any dance contests. I'm not in it to win any sprint records. And after the Tyson fight at least Teddy had the balls to go back on TV and admit that I could fight.

"We almost got to fight Tyson back when he was released from prison and fought Peter McNeeley. But I was with a greedy promoter at the time, Frank Maloney, who wanted a half a million, and I was looking to make a million on the fight, so it never happened. And then we got close again when he [Tyson] ended up fighting Danny Williams, who agreed to take the fight for less money."

"They thought we were cannon fodder," says Collins, wondering aloud if race had anything to do with the total lack of attention paid to his fighter in the days and weeks before the June 11, 2005, bout. "But we had a game plan and we stuck to it. Our game plan was to lean on Tyson and wear him out. Hold him and lean on him for a few rounds until he was tired and frustrated. Everyone we talked to in boxing said the same thing: You get Tyson past the 4th round and he's done. We talked to his old trainer Freddie Roach, who said the same thing."

McBride and Collins set up camp in Boston, with trainer Goody Petronelli, and had only seven weeks and $15,000 to prepare for their dream shot at Tyson. McBride, who had promised his late father Kevin Sr. that he would fight Tyson, took his conditioning seriously from day one.

"We brought in a couple of sparring partners that looked like Tyson," said Collins. "And we worked on getting Kevin in shape. Our first day of camp we went out to run on a route that Rocky Marciano supposedly ran when he fought. We ended up taking a wrong turn and going eight and a half miles. I'm a small guy so I can run all day, but Kevin's 270 pounds. But he never gave up and he never fell out— that's when I knew he was going to be okay."

Conditioning wasn't the only way that Collins conceived to prop up his fighter. Besides the hypnotist, Collins had a friend in journalism print up mock newspaper headlines with words like "Irish Eyes Are Smiling" and "McBride KO's Iron Mike."

"They were the first things that Kevin saw every morning. And in one of the papers, my friend made a photograph of Tyson sitting on his ass in the ring after Kevin knocked him down, with Kevin looking back at him, and I'll be damned if that wasn't the exact thing that happened in the fight, with Tyson slumping down the ropes and sitting on his backside. The only thing that was different was the color of Kevin's trunks.

"At the press conference we wanted Kevin to look as big as possible, just to get close to Tyson and remind him that he was a much smaller man. After they stood toe to toe for the photographs, Tyson walked off the podium first, on his own, which to my knowledge is the only time that's ever happened."

"I told him that when I hit him all of Ireland was going to feel it," says McBride. "He told me I was going to break my hand."

True to his plan, McBride came out and began the task of leaning, holding, and wearing Tyson down. Tyson began the fight with his trademark slips and flurries, but age had taken the zip off the punches, if not the power. Age and a lack of zeal for conditioning also put Tyson at a disadvantage as the fight wore on.

"The first two rounds were a ground war," says Collins. "It was just Kevin trying to tie him up and frustrate him. But then as the fight went on he got more confident . . . he let right hands go, he let left hands go."

"He hit me hard," said McBride. "He's the hardest puncher I've ever faced. But he looked small in the ring. When I met him when we first signed for the fight, he seemed larger than life, with all of the cameras and everything, but in the ring he was very compact."

As the fight progressed, Tyson's tactics became more questionable. McBride was cut by a Tyson headbutt.

"I looked at him in the 6th round, in a clinch, and said, 'Is that all you've got? Because if it is, you're in trouble.' That's when Tyson tried to break my arm."

"Goody [Petronelli] stopped the cut. He's a great cutman. I knew we had to knock him out or get him stopped," said Collins. "It was Tyson's show, and it was clear that our role was just to go in there and be cannon fodder for him. In fact, after Tyson retired on his stool, we were still behind on all of the judges' scorecards. I was sitting behind Kevin in the corner, so I could see across the ring to Tyson's corner, and I saw Fenech telling the referee that Tyson wouldn't be coming out for the 7th round. I immediately started screaming and jumped on Kevin's back!"

Tyson, who would flurry like the Tyson of old in the first 15 to 20 seconds of each round, simply ran out of gas. He also resorted to questionable tactics as he felt the fight slipping away.

"He tried to bite off my nipple at one point," says McBride, with a straight face. "We were in a clinch . . . somewhere there's a great picture of Mike with his mouth around my nipple.

"All the mothers in Ireland lit holy candles for me," says McBride. "And after the fight, I thanked God and thanked my father for the dream come true. Also, somebody backstage said 'Muhammad Ali is leaving and he wants to see Kevin McBride.' Well, I wasn't going to miss that. I gave Muhammad Ali a hug and got to shake his hand. I told him it was the biggest night of my life . . . that I got to meet a legend and beat a legend. Then he pulled me over and whispered something in my ear. Do you know what he said? He said, 'I'm the greatest, but you're the latest.' Money couldn't buy that, you know what I mean?"

WHILE THE TYSON FIGHT opened many doors for McBride, it may not have been the financial windfall they expected, as the McBride camp earned a total of only $150,000 for the fight.

"After taxes, corner fees, training, etc., Kevin only took home about $50,000" says Collins. "But Kevin was treated like the president in Ireland. It's a small country, and he's a hero there. There was a parade shortly after the fight, and they put us in one of those open-topped buses. We got to meet Dennis Leary."

McBride's handlers are eyeing several future opportunities, as it is time for the fighter (who hasn't fought since the Tyson bout in June of 2005) to capitalize.

"We're possibly looking at the winner of the Ruiz versus Valuev fight, or maybe one of the Klitschkos," says Collins. Valuev, a Russian with a 40–0 record who stands over seven feet tall, is an intriguing option. It would be perhaps the largest collection of heavyweight height and girth in boxing history. McBride, however, is fixated elsewhere.

"I want to fight both the Klitschkos on the same night," adds McBride, an idea which elicits only a chuckle from Collins.

Or there is the possibility of fighting Tyson again. Perhaps in Dublin. Perhaps somewhere else in Europe or Asia. Currently Tyson is retired, although rumors abound throughout the boxing community that he is looking for another fight, perhaps against blown-up light heavyweight Antonio Tarver or another opponent.

"I think Tyson can still be dangerous again if he really dedicated himself to training and fighting. He still has the punch and that's the last thing to go. They would love Kevin in China," says Collins. "We'll put him in a gown . . . a kimono . . . whatever it takes."

The camp is looking to capitalize on the first victory and the fact that they have access to a potential boxing goldmine—a white, Irish champion—which they hope to use as a bargaining chip for more dollars this time around. But Collins and McBride have resigned themselves to the fact that they will have to sign with a "big" promoter such as Don King or Bob Arum to have access to real dollars.

"Yeah, maybe we'll make $160k this time," says McBride with a laugh.

"Let me tell you a story," he says, leaning back in his chair. "Before I fought Tyson, Packi says to me, 'Kevin, if you beat Mike Tyson, you'll never have to worry about walking into a store and wondering how much things cost.' He was trying to motivate me. Well, shortly after the Tyson fight, I went into a store to buy some slippers . . . and I picked out a nice pair and just walked them up to the cashier. Do you know how much they were?" he asks, rhetorically. "Seventy dollars! For a pair of slippers. If I'd known that," he adds, "I wouldn't've fuckin' bought 'em."

The waitress has come and gone. Her shift is over, and she stops by our table to leave us the check and tell us that another waitress will be taking over. This one is about 60 years old and far less interesting to McBride. After McBride argues for the check (he wouldn't let me pay for the omelet), there is more playful banter with the waitress. McBride tells her to have sweet dreams, but not to dream about him. Finally, before she goes, he asks, "Do you know who I am?"

The question hangs in the air for what feels like a long moment. Packi Collins and I exchange glances. We are witnessing the arc of fame gained, fame lost, and fame relative; which can sometimes get ugly.

"No, I don't," she responds.

"I'm Kevin McBride," he says, smiling, extending his hand. "I'm the guy that beat Mike Tyson."

ABOUT THE AUTHOR

TED KLUCK is a freelance writer whose work appears regularly on ESPN.com and in the pages of *Sports Spectrum Magazine*, where his column, Pro and Con, received a national award in 2002. He lives in Lansing, MI, with his wife Kristin and son Tristan.

INDEX

Ali, Muhammad, xviii–xix, 13–14, 79, 112, 131, 159, 182, 225, 240
Arlt, Ken, 94, 95

Barkley, Iran, 26
Barry, Kevin, 181
Bellamy, Ronald, 207
Berbick, Trevor, 14, 78, 79–80, 81, 96
Bey, David, 52, 122
Biggs, Tyrell, 109–127, 206, 224, 226
Botha, Francois, 201
Bowe, Riddick, 89, 96, 117, 141, 160, 179, 181–182, 203, 206, 207, 215, 226, 227
Boyd, Lorenzo, 60
Brewster, Lamon, 212, 216
Broad, James, 49, 76
Brock, Calvin, 192
Bruno, Frank, 80
Butler, Lionel, 141
Byarm, Lionel, 181
Byrd, Chris, xvii, 174, 216

Calkins, Clint, 136
Coetzee, Gerrie, 95, 96

Collins, Paschal, 235
Collins, Stevie, 236
Cooney, Gerry, 30
Cummins, Jeff, 63–64

Damiani, Francesco, 116
Davis, Carlton, 117
De Leon, Carlos, 67
Donald, Larry, 174
Douglas, James "Buster," xv, xvi, 100, 138,
    181, 206

Esch, Eric, 131
Etienne, Cliff, xvi, 13
Evans, Mike, 116

Ferguson, Jesse, 158
Foreman, George, 79, 82, 112, 166, 181,
    206, 208
Francis, Julius, 201
Frazier, Joe, xix, 43–45, 47, 52, 53, 113
Frazier, Marvis, 45–58, 78, 113

Gamache, Joey, 5, 8
Gatti, Arturo, 5
Golota, Andrew, 211–219
Grant, Michael, 206
Grant, Uriah, 66
Green, Mitch, xvii, 24, 29, 33–41, 206, 207
Gross, Reggie, 60, 81

Hagler, Marvin, 207
Hearns, Thomas, 223
Hill, Clarence, 137
Hill, Virgil, 114

Holmes, Larry, xviii, 32, 52, 76, 80, 82,
    129–131, 181, 191–192, 193, 225–226
Holyfield, Evander, 82, 96, 102–103, 114,
    121, 131, 169–185, 218, 227, 228
Hosea, William, 60
Hunter, Mike, 158

Jaco, David, 28
Jacobs, Jim, 158
Johnson, Jack, 225

Kurtz, Jim, xvi

Leonard, Sugar Ray, 32, 118
Lewis, Lennox, xvii, xviii, 15, 82, 117, 177,
    204, 216, 221–222, 223–232
Louis, Joe, 159, 208

Mathis, Buster, Jr., 117, 153–167, 203
Mathis, Buster, Sr., 156–157, 158, 159,
    166–167
McBride, Kevin, xvii, 6–7, 9–10, 12, 233–242
McCall, Oliver, 131, 224, 227
McGuigan, Barry, 200
McNeeley, Peter, xvi, 149–151, 237
Mendoza, Gilbert, 141
Mercer, Ray, 230
Mesi, Joe, 39
Minto, Brian, 141
Montiy, Kevin, 6, 236
Moorer, Michael, 179
Morrison, Tommy, 89, 96

Nelson, Conroy, 28
Nielsen, Brian, 13

Norris, Orlin, 140, 201
Norris, Terry, 162

Okine, Abraham, 141

Page, Greg, 138
Pastrano, Willie, 156
Pegues, Jeff, xvii
Peter, Sam, 165
Pryor, Aaron, 143–144

Qawi, Dwight Muhammad, 181

Rachman, Hasim, 224, 227
Ratcliff, Alfonso, 193
Ribalta, Jose, 59–72, 193
Richardson, Ricardo, 66
Rodrigues, Adilson, 30
Ruddock, Donovan, 177
Ruddock, Razor, xvi
Ruiz, John, 179, 216

Savarese, Lou, 166, 199–209
Scaff, Sam, 19–24, 27–32
Seldon, Bruce, xvi, 141
Sims, Jeff, 121
Smith, Chris, 5
Smith, James, xvii, 14, 34, 52, 73–86, 97, 137
Spinks, Leon, xviii
Spinks, Michael, 7, 140, 193
Springs, Ravea, 133
Stevenson, Teofilo, 66, 114, 116

Taylor, Meldrick, 114
Thomas, Pinklon, xvii, 79, 87–107

Tillis, James, 95
Tillman, Henry, xvi, 110, 115
Toney, James, 174
Torres, Jose, 140, 156, 158
Tubbs, Nate, 134
Tubbs, Tony, 52, 113, 133–147
Tucker, Tony, xvi, 14, 140
Turner, West, 31

Vaden, Paul, 162
Vecchione, Vinny, xvi

Waller, Jason, 133, 144–146
Weaver, Mike, 80, 82, 96, 226
Whitaker, Lance, 206
Whitaker, Pernell, 114
Williams, Danny, 237
Williams, Johnny, 66
Williamson, Davarryl, 236
Witherspoon, Tim, 30, 52, 76, 77, 80, 82, 96,
    138, 207
Wofford, Danny, 37

Young, Jimmy, 137